HOW DID YOU FIND ME?

HOW DID YOU FIND ME?

James D. Heintz

iUniverse, Inc.
New York Lincoln Shanghai

HOW DID YOU FIND ME?

iUniverse books may be ordered through booksellers or by contacting:

iUniverse
2021 Pine Lake Road, Suite 100
Lincoln, NE 68512
www.iuniverse.com
1-800-Authors (1-800-288-4677)

The views expressed in this work are solely those of the author and do not necessarily reflect the views of the publisher, and the publisher hereby disclaims any responsibility for them.

ISBN-13: 978-0-595-40461-2 (pbk)
ISBN-13: 978-0-595-84831-7 (ebk)
ISBN-10: 0-595-40461-8 (pbk)
ISBN-10: 0-595-84831-1 (ebk)

Printed in the United States of America

Contents

1

WHY ARE WE HERE?

My sister and I spent six years struggling to understand the disease that victimized our mother. Living with Alzheimer's is like a cross-country trip in a tired, old car. You never know when it's going to break down, and the ride is a painful experience for the driver, and all the passengers. We attempted to bring Mom some degree of relief and happiness, and had many failures, and occasional moments of success.

Early in our roles as caretakers of our Mother we were surprised when Mom's new physician diagnosed her with Alzheimer's. We were aware that she was confused and attributed much of her disorientation to our father's recent death. We had her medical charts transferred from Yakima, Washington to Florence, Oregon where they were appraised and evaluated. As extensive as her records were, Alzheimer's had not been identified as the source of her many disabilities.

With her new diagnosis made we began a process of attempting to understand her disease and found the definition given by the Alzheimer's Association. "Alzheimer's (*AHLZ-high-merz*) disease is a progressive brain disorder that gradually destroys a person's memory and ability to learn, reason, make judgments, communicate and carry out daily activities. As Alzheimer's progresses, individuals may also experience changes in personality and behavior, such as anxiety, suspiciousness or agitation, as well as delusions or hallucinations." Although we were armed with this very accurate definition, my sister and I often found ourselves unprepared both for the pain and loss we experienced and the many, many decisions that were necessary along the way.

For most of my adult life I've found that writing about my experiences proved beneficial in my understanding myself, and often helped in guiding me towards decisions that were positive. I also found that e-mails between my sister and myself, were very therapeutic and gave my sister a better understanding of the daily processes Mom was going through.

My sister, Judy, and I spent lots of time talking with health care professionals and social workers who did their best to guide us towards literature and classes that would educate and support us. With their knowledge and encouragement we did better, but most often we felt ill equipped to deal with our Mother and her disease.

Many people are able to read clinical data and apply it to the problems they are addressing. I have found that hearing or reading about another's personal experience is far more beneficial. Throughout this process I wanted to read someone's story. I wanted to read about a mom like mine and her family. I wanted a story told by someone who had lived with this disease and was willing to tell me about the things I couldn't read on a medical chart of symptoms.

After a couple of years of writing to heal myself and collecting the e-mails I had exchanged with my sister, I realized that others might benefit from my notes, letters and the lessons I painfully recorded as I did my best to keep my Mother under my wing and protection. You will also notice in the early months and years I wrote a great deal and towards the end I often found myself beyond words.

My story begins with some family history and then my father's death. The history is important, because this disease affects family, friends and all the professionals who try to ease the path. My father's death is also important, because that was when Judy and I first observed our mother's behavior apart from him. Dad, as spouses often do, did a great job caring for Mom. He protected her from friends and family by elevating his own vigilance, subtle takeovers of household responsibilities, making excuses for her mistakes, and myriad other things to veil her disease.

2

FAMILY HISTORY

Our parents were hard working middle class people who lived most of their years in Yakima, Washington, a small farming community in the middle of the state. We were always quick to share with visitors our pride at living in the "Fruit Bowl of the Nation."

Dad owned an auto garage in the middle of town and was an excellent mechanic. Around the age of twelve, I started pushing a broom and cleaning up the garage on Saturdays. The fellows that worked for Dad made me feel welcome and taught me a lot about being a man. Everyone called Dad Johnny, and he was known to be good and honest. His voice boomed like Goliath. When customers came into the front, I could easily hear him greeting them jovially, though I was clear in the back end of his shop, where we stored tires and the guys kept all the centerfolds taped to the back of the bathroom walls.

Mom had been a homemaker. She kept her place looking like a showroom in a nice furniture store. She couldn't afford all the things she wanted, and loved it when business was good and she could buy a new chair or table lamp. She liked being a Mom, too. She and Dad had three children; daughter, Judy, the responsible big sister; me, the inventive one; and Steve, the serious one. All three of us kids knew that when we came home, even if it was in the middle of the day, she would be there to care for us. Many were the afternoons when Mom and the other moms would sit on a blanket in our front yard, as a passel of neighborhood kids played around them.

In addition to a close nuclear family, we were blessed with a large and close extended family, always getting together, swapping tales, solving problems, and loving each other. I had grandparents, aunts and uncles, and a bunch of cousins to enrich holidays and everyday life.

My Mom was the oldest of three children. Her brother Don died a couple of years before my father. He had owned a twenty-acre fruit farm outside of Yakima. Uncle Don's farm held some of the best memories of my childhood where we spent long summer days running through orchards, playing in his barn, and in the little red farmhouse he and his wife, Inga, called home. They had two daughters, Nan and Becky.

Mom's younger sister is Katharine. It seemed like Mom and Katharine were always talking to each other. Sometimes they would have little spats and wouldn't visit for a day or two. Most often they enjoyed each other, talking about us kids and their husbands. Katharine is married to Keith. They have three children. Shelly was first, then Kristi, and Jeff.

Our families spent a lot of time together when I was growing up. Every Sunday we would drive out to Mom's parents' house for a big dinner or a weenie roast over Grandpa's fireplace. On Christmases we would go out early, taking all our presents with us, which we piled around the tree with everyone else's until the living room was swallowed up with them. After presents and a huge feast, the women would go in the kitchen to chatter and clean up, and the men would sit around the living room smoking and talking. Although rarely spoken of, a "Code of Family" developed and was understood by all.

Shortly before Dad retired, he and Mom bought a smaller house on Fourteenth Avenue and made it into a cozy home. Mom filled it with her furniture and her prized upright piano. She loved raising us kids, but after we were grown, she kept busy taking care of Dad, the house, her flower gardens and making beautiful music. As the years passed, Mom & Dad's kids scattered, and time with children, and grandchildren, dwindled to fluttering visits with lots of chatter and laughter and too little time. Mom persisted in complaining about the loss of that big family that she had always known and loved. It was a loss to her, as it was to all those in the next generation who missed out on that irreplaceable closeness. Instead of staying in the Yakima Valley like Mom and her siblings, my sister and I "scattered." We moved to California and Oregon shortly after our marriages.

Like my Mom, my sister, Judy, is a homemaker. She lives in Sacramento, California with her husband, Mag. He's retired and made his living building cabinets. He had learned his trade in Norway where he was born and raised. They have three sons, Greg, Brian and Lee.

My brother Steve was a couple of years younger than myself and was convinced that life was always going to be difficult. Mom said he put a lot of effort into making sure it was. He died the year before my father, and missed out on the rough road Judy and I traveled with our mother. Steve had two daughters Jackie and Erica, who had different moms, and a step-son, Brandon. All of them, like most of us, had a hard time understanding their dad. And we miss him.

I've lived in Florence, Oregon for the past seven years with my wife, Suzanne. I have two children from my first marriage, Jamie and Jordan. Suzanne has a son named Jason, who lives in Arizona. I'm proud of the kids in our family. They have educated themselves and are working in professions they find fulfilling. Jamie is married to Gregg and has a five-year old son, Skylar. They live in Springfield. Jordan is married to Erica, and lives in Portland.

We were a pretty typical American family, probably a lot like yours. Though off in different directions and living our own lives, times come when family is family and it's like a gathering of eagles. Such a time was at hand for us.

3

THE STORY BEGINS

MARCH

March 28, 2000

"This isn't real. I can't believe it. This just isn't real." I have heard my Mama's words repeated again and again over the past twelve days. Early Tuesday morning the phone rang. It wasn't time to get up and too early for a business call. Suzanne, my loving wife, for less than seven months, answered and I heard her say, "Hi, Judy. Oh, when did it happen?" I was out of our bed and into the bathroom using the door and walls to protect my ears from hearing the rest of her words.

Mom and Dad are in there eighties, with Dad, at eighty-three, a few years older than Mom. We have watched Mom's health slip over the past few years, and Dad has accepted more and more of the household responsibilities. Mom has resisted his control, yet allowed it to occur. She has known on some level that she was having a hard time doing lots of things. Dad didn't complain and was patient with her. He's old school and is slow to discuss his problems with us kids. By nature he keeps our topics of conversation political or light hearted. A few days ago I had asked Dad, "Are you doing OK? Do we need to find you some help to deal with Mom?" He was quick with a, "Its OK, Son. I don't feel a need for any help, at this time anyway." Dad had a deep and rich voice that soothed concerns. I was comforted and knew that all was well in his capable hands.

Most of the family was expecting Mom to fall and hurt herself or have a stroke like her mother. "It's John," said Mag. Judy had been unable to continue her conversation with Suzanne and had turned the phone over to her husband. "He had a massive stroke and is in the hospital." "Honey, it's your daddy. He has had a stroke." Suzanne's words smashed through the barrier of door and wall. "Dad? How can it be Dad? He is strong as a bear and healthy." My thoughts swirled as I absorbed the information. "Tell them that we are on our way." I heard the day's first words escape my mouth and felt the emotional armor drop around my body.

Man of Steel. When my brother Steve died, at his own hand fourteen months ago, I watched my father drape armor over himself. He kept his armor on, and did not allow a chip or scratch to develop in it as the months passed. I cried a lot over Steve, but found that today I was following Dad's lead. Today I was choosing to be a man of steel.

Suzanne and I quickly gathered together the things we would need for a week or so in Yakima and loaded the car. I took my blue suit out of my closet and packed it. There may be a funeral to attend. We opened the rear hatch of the car and called the dog into his traveling spot. Elway liked going places. Today, I would have preferred anything else.

The drive was quick. We had an audio book about some fellow's trip across Borneo and it served well as a mental distraction. I drove past the family home in Yakima and turned west on Tieton Drive. We were close to the hospital and I felt myself adjusting my emotional plates of steel. I didn't know what I would experience within the walls of the hospital, and I wanted to be prepared for the worst.

The large sliding glass doors opened. There were several sets of them that keep the weather out and the hospital's climate controlled. Suzanne gathered the room number at the front desk, as I entered the elevator. I pushed the third floor button and again checked my armor. The doors opened and I stepped out. "It must be down this hall," were my words as Suzanne moved in close beside me and held my arm. The bed curtains were open and my cousin Shawn and his new girl friend were sitting beside the bed. I couldn't see Dad until I entered the room. Shawn was holding his hand and Dad was tossing about. I stepped close and captured Dad's eyes with mine. I felt that I had just made contact with a boxer who had been dropped to the mat with an upper cut. His eyes were glazed and searching for anything that would give him orientation. Clank … clank. The armor tightened. Shawn slid back and I took Dad's hand and watched.

I talked with Shawn and my other room companions for an hour until the Neurologist arrived. He put Dad through a series of simple tests and, in a professional and compassionate manner, explained that Dad had the bulk of his working mind destroyed by a blood clot and that he would never recover. When the Doctor finished talking with us, I was left with the hope that my father would die. My father would never talk, walk, hug, or counsel with me again. My father, as the man I loved and admired, would never be accessible to me again.

Shawn, who was sitting beside his girlfriend Elizabeth, found the Doctor's words unacceptable. "He knows I'm here. He is responding to my touch. See how he squeezes my hand when I squeeze his. Watch his eyes when I talk with him. He knows I'm here." My sweet Dad was temporally captured by his body, which had left him confused and unable to process the world he knew so well. God willing he will quickly find freedom. God willing!

Like country folk the family filled the hospital. Dad's room was occupied, from sunrise to late at night, by friends, family, priests and occasional medical staff. When the family left to sleep there were always one or two in his room for the night watch. We didn't want him to die alone.

March 29, 2000

Day two was hard for Dad. He wanted to understand and fought with us as he explored his body that had been left half useless by his stroke. He had the power of a young man and alone he would have deposited himself on the tile floor. We frustrated and distracted him, until morphine was again administered and his bewildered mind was soothed. He would remain calm for a couple of hours and then he would again begin the process of exploration, tugging at the tubes that carried in nourishment, oxygen, and drugs. We were tired at the end of this day and were told that as strong as Dad was, his life could last for weeks without support. It seemed a poor reward for a good man.

March 30, 2000

Something calmed Dad on day three. The endless efforts to leave his bed passed. The exploration slowed to rolling sheet edges. His eyes closed and would only slightly open for loud noises and then not at all. A squeeze would not be returned and rolling in search of comfort passed to motionlessness.

My mother talked to him for a little while. She was close to his face and rubbed his bare shoulder. Her words were soothing and personal. We all watched her with him. We saw what had kept them together for over sixty-two years.

We didn't go away. The nurses complimented us and said, "We were a nice family and all seemed to be on the same page." They had to climb over us to attend to Dad's needs and didn't seem to mind. On night three our cousin Nan slept in the bed next to Dad's for the night watch.

March 31, 2000

Springtime in Yakima is impressive with the soft breezes, hills covered with light green velvet and blue skies with cotton rich clouds. My sister experienced the best the valley had to offer every morning. She rose with or before the sun and drove to our father's side. There were few hours that she wasn't beside him. We watched her. She watched him. We worried about her. She worried about him. The fourth day was like the rest for Judy. When she arrived at her post beside our Dad, he was calm. His entire day was calm. His body was at rest and would not respond to us. We all enjoyed that day with Dad. There was lots of laughter and we were inconsiderate of other patients who had wanted peace and quiet. We were all lost in each other, in loving each other and in being beside Dad. He wouldn't move a muscle, but we all knew that he was, on a spiritual level, enjoying his family. I talked with Dad that night. I told him that all was in order. That he had done a good job preparing for this time, and that Mom was going to be OK. I said, "Dad, you can go! It's all taken care of."

Judy went home. We all went home. Nan climbed into the extra bed for a few hours, then called her mom to take over for her. She had worked hard during the day, and needed a good night's sleep. Inga took her night watch. Who would spend the night watching Dad wasn't discussed. We all seemed to know what needed doing, and it was done.

APRIL

April 1, 2000

Dad's breathing had been deep and regular. Liquid in his lungs could be heard and we knew that it was the voice of "the old man's friend." Inga heard a change in his breath and called the nurse to check. She cleared his throat and said, "He should be more comfortable now." He was. Two breaths later he died.

"James? Your father has passed away." The ring of the phone at 5:30 a.m. was the first announcement of my father's passing. My aunt, Inga's words only confirmed the event. The night before the nurse had talked about the strength of Dad's body and that we shouldn't be surprised if he lived for several weeks. He didn't.

Mom cried and cried. She couldn't get out of bed. Suzanne stayed with her, as I headed for the hospital.

Early morning drives are pleasant. The traffic is light and the sky is slightly illumined by the on coming sun. I keyed my cell phone and called my son. He was in Los Angeles sleeping and knew that the ring was a death announcement. I had been a man of steel for most of the week and was unable to share more than, "He has died son. My daddy has died." Another call to my daughter's answer machine and I was in the parking lot of the hospital.

You don't get to enter the hospital's main entrance early in the morning. The only public entry is through the emergency rooms. The security officer was in place and glanced at me over his clipboard as I walked past him towards the elevator. I would have been cooperative if he had stopped me. He probably could tell by my face that I was barely containing a wave of tears.

Elevator doors opened, closed and then opened again on Dad's floor. I knew well the way and observed that there were few staff and no patients about. Walking down the long hall I saw my Aunt Inga standing outside Dad's door. She moved towards me and said, "Hi, James. I am so sorry." I hardly paused as I accepted my first condolence. She needed a condolence of her own. She had loved and known my father many more years than I. I thanked her, and she walked on down the hall.

I stood in the room beside my father's body. He looked like he did when I left him last night, except he didn't move. He was warm. I held his hand and stroked his bald head. "Aww, Dad. I love you." The words slashed into my armor and threatened to release the weeping it contained.

I am a Baha'i and there were spiritual things that I wanted to do with my father before he died and now with his body. They are important things that are close to my inner core and are personal between my Creator and myself. In Dad's third day I read many prayers as I held his hand. My sister sat to the side and watched. It was just the three of us and the words I read brought comfort. Now it was time for the prayers for the departed, special prayers that would not have been appropriate until this moment.

I expected family to flock to his deathbed. No one came. The time was mine and it was a gift from God. I opened my prayer book and read. There are many prayers for the departed and words like "cause them to enter the garden of happiness, cleanse them with the most pure water, and grant them to behold Thy splendors on the loftiest mount" that gave me great solace. After two hours beside Dad I asked the nurse to bring me a tub of warm water and I slowly washed his body, his face and I closed his eyes. I washed his chest, arms and his massive hands. Over and over I thanked God for the love this body had given. As I finished my task nature began claiming my father's body. I folded my washcloth and stepped back for my last gaze at him.

Life continues to provide me with new experiences and growth. I have never purchased a grave site or arranged for a funeral. April 1, 2000, I did both. The visit to the cemetery was good. I went with Suzanne, and with her support, selected a site near Mom's parents. We purchased two plots and were happy with the location. I asked the manager if I could participate with the gravediggers in filling Dad's grave. They said, "Yes, you can do that if you wish, sir." "I wish," was my reply.

Our next visit was the funeral home and Suzanne, Judy and I attended to this task. Charles, the young, black-suited man, was our consultant. They may have another title for his job but consultant is the best I can come up with. Charles did a good job for us. We buried Dad in a modestly priced coffin with no additional muss or fuss. He would have been proud of us.

On the second day of Dad's hospitalization, my sister called Father Edward from St. Paul's Cathedral Church. It was the church we had all attended as children, and Father Edward had been my fifth grade basketball coach. He came by to see Dad and gave him his Catholic Last Rights. Judy and I liked the priest's visit and later called him to ask if he would conduct Dad's funeral. He had other commitments, but set them aside at our request, and fulfilled our desires.

April 3, 2000

"I just can't do it. John wouldn't ask me to do something this difficult," were Mom's words. She knew that she did not have the spirit or stamina for today's task. Suzanne offered to care for her and the rest of us left for church.

It was several hours before the funeral and Father Edward wanted to spend some time with us to learn more about Dad. Discussing Dad is like talking about a vintage car. While appreciating the beauty of the machine, you also knew that some parts were held in place with bailing wire. Dad's life wasn't perfect, but he loved easily and liked people.

The grandchildren carried the body of their grandpa. They were all young women and men and they loved him. Several knew him well while others knew him less. They were serious with their task. Faces that knew lightness and laughter were somber. They carried him to the front door of the church, and there they placed their trust on wooden supports. They all stepped to the side and allowed Judy and I to spread the pall over Dad's coffin. We then rolled him to the front of the chapel where his body lay in the center of the gathering.

Catholic traditions were practiced. Prayers were said, incense burned, holy water sprinkled, words of praise and respect were spoken and an angelic-voiced woman sang songs, as organ music filled the chapel with the breath of God. Again we rolled him to the church doors and opened them to the brightness of the day, where the grandchildren again shared their load and carried Dad's casket to the hearse. The funeral was done. We were all pleased.

The drive through town was filled with little white cars with flashing lights parting the traffic to deliver us to the cemetery. Old men often have small funerals. Dad's was large. He seemed to capture the hearts of young and old. I liked that about him.

Jamie, Jackie, Erica, Greg, Bryan, Brandon and Lee carried John Martin Heintz for the last time and set his coffin on the straps that covered the green draped grave that would hold his remains forever. Father Edward talked a bit more and blessed Dad's grave. He then stepped back and relinquished the balance of our goodbye's to friends and family. We talked about him and told little stories about his powerful hugs, big heart, booming voice, hard work, great counsel and friendship. Some of our words were inadequate and some eloquent. Finally we stopped talking and friends got in their cars and returned to their daily living. Many of the close family remained.

I signaled the staff to begin the burial. From storage garages below our knoll, small yard trucks came with trailers and tractors. Uniformed grounds keepers removed the grass carpet and lowered Dad's coffin into its vault. Quickly one keeper dropped into the grave and placed six slabs across the top of the vault and as quickly jumped back to the surface. At his nod, I took my shovel and lifted dirt. I cast it upon the vault, and then did it again and again. Soon Shawn joined me, followed by my brother-in-law, Mag. Slowly we continued our task as my sister, cousins, nieces and nephews tossed shovel after shovel of dirt upon the grave until it was filled with a slight mound. The keeper placed the sod upon the dirt. Together we tamped with our feet until all the new cut edges of the grass were closed and it was hard to tell that we had just opened the earth and closed it holding the body of my Dad. I loved the purity of burying Dad. I loved knowing where his body is and how it got there. I loved closing this chapter of my life with dirt on my hands. I love my Father.

4

DAD'S OBITCH

◆

(Mom's humor for obituaries)

John (Johnny) Heintz, 83 passed away April 01, 2000 at Memorial Hospital a few miles from his birthplace on North 32nd Avenue. Johnny was born November 25, 1916 on his parents' fruit farm. His parents were Russian German immigrants who had lived most of their young adult lives wheat ranching in Canada. He was their seventh child and the only one born in the United States.

John's stories of his childhood farm life were rich and endless.

In his early 20's Johnny worked in his big brother, Joe's bakery in Naches. It was there that he met, courted and on June 9th, 1939 married his wife, Virginia McDowell. Together John and Virginia had three children. Judy Myre of Sacramento, California, James Heintz of Florence, Oregon and Steve Heintz who last year preceded his father to God's Great Garden. Judy, James and Steve gave Johnny and Virginia eight wonderful grandchildren. John's older sisters, Theresa and Mary, will miss their little brother.

Johnny served in WWII and was stationed in Japan for the early occupation. He was a Staff Sergeant, who cooked for the troops and was nick named "the old man" due to his entering the service in his mid-twenties. Most of his work life was involved in the service of automobiles and trucks. He was a skilled mechanic, who managed stations for Standard, owned and operated the 10th Avenue Mobil Service, and then Clarks's Philips 66 Service, on Fifth and West Yakima Avenue. At the end of his working career he taught small engine mechanics at J.M. Perry Technical Institute. As a boss, educator and friend, Johnny was easily described as "a hell of a good guy."

Funeral services for Johnny will be held on Sunday, April 03 at 10:00 a.m. at Shaw & Son's Funeral Home.

5

MOM ON HER OWN

By the time my sister and I dealt with the problems attached to the death of our father and directed our attention more fully towards our mother, we realized that she was far from OK. Several months later, after we had exposed ourselves to the information provided by the Alzheimer's Association, we knew that our mother had already passed through the first five of the seven stages of the disease.

Stage 1: No Impairment (normal function)

Unimpaired individuals experience no memory problems and none are evident to a health care professional during a medical interview.

Stage 2: Very mild cognitive decline (may be normal age related changes or earliest signs of Alzheimer's disease)

Individuals may feel as if they have memory lapses, especially in forgetting familiar words or names or the location of keys, eyeglasses or other everyday objects. But these problems are not evident during a medical examination or apparent to friends, family or co-workers.

Stage 3: Mild cognitive decline

Early-stage Alzheimer's can be diagnosed in some, but not all, individuals with these symptoms. Friends, family or co-workers begin to notice deficiencies. Problems with memory or concentration may be measurable in clinical testing or discernible during a detailed medical interview. Common difficulties include:

- Word or name finding problems noticeable to family or close associates.
- Decreased ability to remember names when introduced to new people.
- Performance issues in social or work settings noticeable to family, friends or co-workers.

- Reading a passage and retaining little material.
- Losing or misplacing a valuable object.
- Decline in ability to plan or organize.

Stage 4: Moderate cognitive decline (Mild or early-stage Alzheimer's disease)

At this stage, a careful medical interview detects clear-cut deficiencies in the following areas:

- Decreased knowledge of recent occasions or current events.
- Impaired ability to perform challenging mental arithmetic for example, to count backward from 100 by 7s.
- Decreased capacity to perform complex tasks, such as marketing, planning dinner for guests or paying bills and managing finances.
- Reduced memory of personal history.
- The affected individual may seem subdued and withdrawn, especially in socially or mentally challenging situations.

Stage 5: Moderately severe cognitive decline (Moderate or mid-stage Alzheimer's disease)

Major gaps in memory and deficits in cognitive function emerge. Some assistance with day-to-day activities becomes essential. At this stage, individuals may:

- Be unable during a medical interview to recall such important details as their current address, their telephone number or the name of the college or high school from which they graduated.
- Become confused about where they are or about the date, day of the week, or season.
- Have trouble with less challenging mental arithmetic; for example, counting backward from 40 by 4s or from 20 by 2s.
- Need help choosing proper clothing for the season or the occasion.
- Usually retain substantial knowledge about themselves and know their own mane and the names of their spouse or children.
- Usually require no assistance with eating or using the toilet.

May 15, 2000

"Oh, Mama! Why does it have to be so difficult?" My mother is grieving the death of her husband, my father. He died six weeks ago. Mom has been dependent upon Dad for several years. He did almost everything for her. He cooked, cleaned, shopped, and helped her in and out of the tub and lots of other personal services I don't know about. He paid the bills, mowed the lawn, and fixed the broken plumbing. Two months ago he was under the house clearing a sewer drain.

My sister Judy and I spent weeks checking out assisted living housing and other facilities in Yakima that help folks who need help. Suzanne and I had discussed bringing Mom home with us when we were driving to Yakima for Dad's death. We had thought that she could live with us or we could set her up in one of the local assisted living centers in Florence, Oregon where we lived. Judy, who lives in Sacramento, said that she and Mag had gone through the same process. Around our father's deathbed Mom's sister and other family members expressed their concern over our thoughts of moving Mom out of the valley. We all talked and agreed that she would live out her life in Yakima.

We were drawing close to a placement when Nan, our cousin, offered to care for Mom. Nan is the daughter of my mother's brother who died last year. She cared for him and thought that she would like to do the same for Mom. It pleased both Judy and I that we wouldn't have to move Mom out of her home, and that she would be with family.

Having to learn to sleep alone after sixty-one years and having your lifetime companion gone is a lot to adjust to. When a young niece has been placed in charge of you, and what happens in your home, life becomes intolerable.

My Mama has always been strong and opinionated. She was very responsible as a wife and mother. She also did what she wanted when she wanted. Beside the aggressive side of Mom there was also a public shyness. She was very slow, if not immobile, when it came to her involvement with activities outside of her home and family. I had often encouraged her to volunteer her time, but her reply never varied, "It's hard for me to meet new people and do new things." I would pressure her, as young men often do their mothers, and she would appease me with, "OK, I will think about it."

Before Dad retired, most of his energy was directed towards work and activities outside of the home. Mom was in complete charge of the house. All Dad had to do was take out the garbage and mow the lawn. When he retired, he started a new program, which increased his involvement in the household operations.

These plans infringed upon Mom's well-established turf and she hated it. Dad was unstoppable and claimed more and more of Mom's work. The last years before his death, Dad had attained his goal and was king of the house. Mom did nothing and sat around complaining about Dad being so bossy. I never considered that taking more responsibility may not have been my father's choice, but a necessity.

Today my sister and I are forced to reconsider Mom's living conditions. She is mildly demented with both of her oars working most of the time. Her problems have to do with the times when one or both of those oars are out of the water. The complaints about bossiness that she had lodged against Dad transformed into the same complaints about Nan.

Mom believes that her processing is OK. She puts fresh food in the garbage, and the garbage in the refrigerator. She skillfully hides her purse, and then we spend hours looking for it. She wants to cook, but goes out to water her flowers with the burner hot under an empty pan. She wants to run her own life and can't. She refuses to accept her limitations and is directing her frustrations and anger towards Nan.

Judy and I believe that Nan, after only a couple of weeks on Mom's turf, has reevaluated her offer and wishes that she had kept her old job. She is still hanging in there, but we all know, and understand, that her commitment has worn thin and may soon vanish.

This period of transition has given Judy and I time between the trauma of Dad's death and having to uproot Mom. We are thankful for this minor plus, but we are back to placing our Mom in a home which is not hers. Shit!

Thanks Mom for offering up your life for us. Thanks for spending your days loving and nurturing us. Thanks for always making us number one in your consideration of everything. Thanks Mom. Oh, by the way Mom. We have decided to place you in an old folks' home. It's your reward from your children for all that you have done for us.

Oh, God! Why does it have to be so difficult? I have found myself thinking, with guilt, that she should have died with Dad. Her tomorrows have no possibility of happiness no matter what we do. She would be unhappy living with us and she hates living with Nan. She will dislike living wherever she lives. "Shit!" I really do want to believe that I am a good son, and today I don't.

6

FIRST OF THE E-MAILS

MAY

Judy and I knew that Mom couldn't be left alone. Having her live at home with either one of us wasn't a realistic option, although we both struggled with a wish that somehow one of us could make our home hers. Finding Mom a safe and happy place became our primary goal and we began our research and kept each other posted with many e-mails and phone calls.

May 16, 2000

Good Morning James,

Did you sleep well last night or are you overwhelmed? I talked with Katharine last night. She spent yesterday with Mom. She felt that both mentally and physically Mom is getting worse quickly. She is becoming more out of touch with reality and more unsure on her feet. Hopefully a change will bring an improvement. We are in for a hot week. The predictions are for 104 to 108 degrees. We do have hot summers! Talk to you soon.

Love, Judy

May 20, 2000

Hi James,

We are moving right along. I'll try and fill you in on the information I have gotten. As for Sacramento, "residential living," as they call it here, starts at $1800.00 a month. I have information on specific places coming. I haven't actually seen any places yet. As for Yakima, there is a place with openings that also sounds interesting. It's located on 96th Avenue and has seven acres. The clients share bedrooms and they house five ladies at the most. The lady, who runs it, is a LPN who specializes in dementia care. She keeps her ladies busy with outings, such as drives, visits to the mall, picnics, walks, even overnight trips when she can. She works with hobbies and crafts. It is a farm environment with animals and costs $1500.00 per month. I haven't seen the place yet. The lady from the hospital is working with me. She is great. There are other places available but the Florence place sounded very promising, too. James, I don't have any set ideas as to where Mom should live. I think there are pros and cons whichever way we go. I was thinking of asking Katharine to check out the Yakima place, but, like you, I wanted to talk first. Does Mom know we are moving her? I haven't talked to her since I talked with you. Bye for now,

Judy

7

MOVING TO FLORENCE, OREGON

JUNE

June 2, 2000

"Judy, I have found a great foster home and they have an opening," were my words. Florence had several foster homes and Serenity Place was on the top of the referral list. I had contacted the owners and followed up with a great visit. It was warm, quilted, flowered and smelled of fresh baked bread. Barbara Williams is the woman we all hope will be there to care for us when we can't do it for ourselves. I made arrangements to drive to Yakima, fetch Mom, and deliver her for an interview the following Tuesday.

The trip to Yakima takes nine hours. Suzanne and I left Florence in the early morning, dropped by Eugene for a delightful Fathers Day breakfast with my daughter Jamie, and arrived in Yakima around seven in the evening. Mom was very happy to see us and very excited to be getting out of town and away from Nan. She was also disappointed with her sister, Katharine, who had tried to talk her into modifying her poor treatment of her niece. We gave Nan her long-awaited relief, and spent the night getting Mom ready for the long trip home.

By 10:00 a.m. we were on the road and Mom loved the drive. She admired the changes in the land as we made our way south. Mom was charmed with our little town and the coastal landscape. I spent Monday working, while Suzanne took Mom and her son, Jason, to the Newport Aquarium. All the travel and the adventure filled Mom with sparkle. She said, "Honey, why can't I just stay with you. I won't be any trouble, and, if you want, I will do the cooking."

It had been two years since Dad had banned Mom from the kitchen, due to the probability that she would burn the house down. "Oh, Mom, I can't let you live here. Suzanne and I have to work, and it wouldn't be good to leave you here alone. You would be afraid and could hurt yourself," were my words. Mom argued a little and then accepted the logic of my position.

The visit with the Williams went well Tuesday and we made arrangements to move Mom in at 11:00 a.m. Thursday. I was delighted with my success in getting her into a wonderful living environment where she could spend the rest of her life with bliss and my daily visits.

"I don't want to do this James. I want to move back home," she said. I presumed that Mom was doing a normal fear-of-change routine, and was confident that within a few days she would find pleasure in the love offered at Serenity Place. Mom's placement went as expected, and she seemed settled as I left and returned to my work.

I had hung her cloths, filled her drawers, and put pictures on her dresser. "Looks pretty cozy doesn't it Mom?" I said. She responded with, "It's OK. I don't think I will need to be here long though." I had no idea at all how prophetic her statement was.

The Williams's had said they expected adjustment problems for several months and would help Mom work through these difficult times. I was impressed with their wisdom and dedication. I felt good about this placement and basked in my sister's praise that I had done a good job.

In an effort to share my perceived success, I wrote this simulated "letter from Mom" to my sister, based on Mom's comments and shifts in perceptions about her new life.

Virginia Heintz
Florence, Oregon 97439

Dear Daughter,

I love my new place in Oregon. The foster home I live in, with three other delightful, old women, is very nice. There are lots of quilts, pillows and beautiful flower arrangements everywhere. The people that own Serenity Place, that's the name of this hellhole, are also delightful. There's a little dog, that looks to be a weenie, and is always sitting on my lap. He looks like the kind of dog that would pee in the corner.

The home is very close to the ocean. If they would cut the twenty acres of coastal pine trees down on the backside of this property, I would be able to see the damn ocean. The days have been cool and the wind blows like hell. I asked

James if I could stay with him in his house, and he said that I would be much happier here. The kid never knew anything, and probably never will.

One of the ladies here is one hundred and two. You can see right through her. She's nothing but skin, bones and too much make up. She does talk, and likes to walk. I think that she and I will get along OK.

I loved the drive from Yakima to Florence. This is a beautiful little town and there are so many tall trees. I can hear the sound of the ocean. I think its sound will help me to fall asleep.

James says that if the wind is blowing in the right direction you can hear the surf at his house. I think that he is right on this, because I heard it yesterday when we were there. Yesterday Suzanne took me to the Newport Aquarium while James worked. You can walk under the tanks and see the fish from the bottom up. I always wondered what it would be like to be a fish and now I know. I had fun.

Well, I don't want to talk forever. Write to me. I don't like being away from the family, and I miss you.

Your Mother

June 3, 2000

Dear Sister,

You may have guessed that Mom didn't write this letter and you are right. I do think that I did a pretty good job of reading her mind. Mom is adjusting. These are difficult changes, and she dislikes change. Today was her first day in her new digs. I set her room up with stuff she likes, hung up her cloths and filled her drawers. I also made sure that she had an ample supply of Tootsie Roll Pops. In time, I feel sure that she will be as happy as possible.

James,

Dotty, one of Mom's new housemates said, "She is giving up, isn't she?" Dotty has lived three years with the Williams, and knew how to make the best of the life offered to the old. She walks three times each day, and likes the William's kid. Her eighty-seven years have left her with Alzheimer's and a broken tailbone. She often smiles when she shares information with you, and she knows the answers to most of the questions she asks. She looks at me with her knowing eyes, relaxes her face and smiles, as I raise my hands in an unknowing gesture to her quiz.

Today Mom seems more compliant. We took a little drive, sat by the ocean for a while, and I showed her the spot on the sand dunes where Suzanne and I married a year ago. We liked being together and she shared her chicken sandwich with me. I always have to eat a little of her food, so she can continue her mothering and help to keep me big and strong. Upon returning, we walked and she complained about her walker. I didn't get mad today. Today, I was compliant, like Mom.

Judy responded to the "Letter from Mom" with the following email:

James,

I just read your Mom letter. Cracked me up. It does sound like her. I bet you are right on target. You didn't get a call during the night did you? So far OK! I have been thinking about all of you a lot. I know caring for Mom isn't easy. Life shouldn't wind down like this. Does Mom need help with her bathroom chores now? I was wondering why they were charging Mom an extra $100.00 a month for pads. She was taking care of herself a couple of months ago.

Today is more yard work! Good Luck. I am sure it will be difficult for all of you! Give Mom a hug for me!

Love, Judy

The look on Barbara's face was the same expression my wife had on her face when she told me, with the phone against her chest, that my father had a massive stroke. The message Barbara had to share was different. "James, I am fearful that our caring for your mother isn't going to work out. She is in much worse shape than I realized. She behaves so differently than she did for our assessment interview last Tuesday." Barbara told me about Mom's inability to follow directions, her forgetfulness, instability on her feet, inability to dress herself, and her high level of confusion.

Mom had been a little unstable and was mildly forgetful for the six days we had spent together and I didn't understand what had happened in the past thirty hours? I got Mom's coat on and we went outside for a walk with her walker. She hated the walker and tried to push it to the side as we moved down the street. "Mom, you have got to use your walker. You will fall without it," I said. "Bossy,

bossy, bossy. Every one in my life is bossy. All day long people are bossing me around and making me do things that they want me to do," were her words.

I got angry with my mother on that walk. She had blown her opportunity to stay in the family home by having a power struggle with her niece. She was going to do the same thing with the Serenity Place people. I wanted happiness for her, and wanted to find a joyful place for her to spend her old age. She and her bull-headedness were going to deny me the feelings of being the good son, again.

We talked a lot on that walk. Mom made I-don't-like-you faces at me. I told her that being mean wasn't going to get her back home, and that back home couldn't happen. We also talked about her sabotaging her opportunity to live in a nice home-like environment, and that she was going to end up in some institutional place that she wouldn't like at all.

Mom remained mad and cried over my not taking her away. Barbara said, "We will watch her over the weekend, and we will talk again Monday." She didn't look hopeful.

June 4, 2000

Sweet Sister,

I just talked with the Williams at Serenity Place. They are not yet ready to give up. Some progress is being made, and Mom is being more helpful. Suzanne is going to take her to visit our local nursing home, which is a classic you-don't-want-to-be-here-place. We are hopeful that this visit will motivate her to greater improvements. I will be taking Mom to the doctor on Wednesday. I pressured the office for an immediate visit. The Williams have a long list of concerns, and we feel that they need to be addressed now.

Jamie came by herself yesterday and visited with Mom. We were in Portland, taking Suzanne's son to the airport, and didn't get home until 9:00 p.m. We did see Jamie for a few minutes before she drove back to Eugene, but I didn't see Mom at all yesterday. I will go out later today. I hope you had a nice weekend and that the heat isn't bothering you. It's seventy-three degrees here and may get up another degree or two. Eugene is in the nineties. I love you sister.

James

Hi James,

I talked to my friend, Gail, today. Mom is behaving much like her Mom did. Being bossed was a problem for her mom, too. After talking to Gail, it seems Mom's behavior is probably not within her control. The good and bad behavior seems to fit the sad pattern. I was glad to hear that the Williams were going to work with Mom longer, and also glad to hear that she will be getting a medical evaluation. I hope things work out in Oregon, but as a back up, do you want me to call the place I was looking at in Yakima? At the time I was getting info, they had two openings. Actually, Gail has had experience with this place. Her mom stayed there for a while. I sure hope Mom can adapt to her Oregon home. It sounds like a nice living situation. Good Luck tomorrow.

Love, Judy

8

BACK TO MY HOUSE

June 5, 2000

For three days Mom attempted to settle into life in a foster home. The owners of the foster home were great. They did a lot to make Mom feel at home, and were unsuccessful. She hated the place and felt very confined. She said, "I can't do anything right here. They boss and boss me. I want to go home." Barbara called me when Mom filled a bag with some of her stuff and was walking away. She said that they just couldn't keep her there not knowing if she was going to slip out the door when they weren't watching. I had the feeling that they didn't need to worry about Mom quietly slip out a door. If she was going to leave, I was sure she would do it with a bit of flair. Looks like I will bring Mom home until I can find another place.

"I want to go home. Oh please James, let me go home." Mom has been with Suzanne and I for three days. There isn't a positive spark in her. She has fallen into the deepest pit of despair. The foster home placement failed. She took all their efforts of support and viewed them as bossing. Mom hates needing help. She hates it that she has so little control over her life. What would a good son do? I so wish I could find some way to lift her spirits, to bring some sparkle into her life. In the past I had a magic touch with Mom. There was something in our relationship that made it possible for me to easily please her. It has always been there, and now its gone. When I asked the Senior Services case manager if Mom was going to be mad at me forever, she said, "No. Someday she won't even know who you are." The thought that I will never again be able to work my magic with Mom is sad. I do not like this path. It's too rough and is hurting us all. I want a different choice. I wish for Mom, Dad's death, which was quick, easy and respectful.

What we are doing here feels mean. If I could think, for a moment, that Mom wasn't along for this spiral to hell, I would feel differently, but she is along and her suffering is extreme. For her there is no port in the storm. No safe shelter. She is exposed to all the harsh elements and I can't pull her into safety.

Over Mom's tears at breakfast I asked her, "Mom, is there something you can think of that you feel happy about?" Her pause was long, and when she turned and looked at me her answer was, "No."

June 23, 2000

Hi James,

Sorry, I didn't get back to you this morning. I just read your mail. My gut feeling would be to hang in there with Oregon at this point in time. I would expect that Mom is not going to be happy any place. Perhaps only time will give us a true picture of what is the best thing to do. If today doesn't work out, I would think it best to try some of the others places you had in mind. I trust your judgment. I hope by bringing up financial considerations I didn't add to your frustrations. That was not my intent. I probably should have said nothing for now. You have enough frustrations going. My thought was that the more we know about this change, the easier it will be. No surprises. Hopefully you will come home with an OK for Mom! I am trying to think positive.

Love, Judy

June 25, 2000

Hi James,

Just wanted to let you know that Mag and I are going up to the cabin tomorrow. We will be back Sunday. If I don't answer mail right away, that is the reason! Talk to you soon.

Love, Judy

9

THE MOVE TO SIUSLAW CARE CENTER

June 28, 2000

The Williams gave up on Mom. We brought her back to our home for several days, then I moved her to the Siuslaw Care Center. It's the same institutional nursing home Suzanne and Mom visited in hopes Mom would appreciate the foster home. Rather than rejecting the care center, she responded positively to the new environment, at first. She had hated the feeling of being in close quarters. This place was open and would give her lots of moving room. The foster home was easily recognizable to her as a "home." The care center, however, was so large that she imagined herself in lots of different places. It was a home, a hospital, a hotel, a restaurant. As she moved from place to place, she had a sense of travel and exploration. Things are looking up!

During her time with the Williams, we took Mom and her medical records from Yakima to a local physician who dealt with the elderly. She was diagnosed with Alzheimer's. Mom couldn't tell what day it was, the time, hour or who was President. She was embarrassed by the doctor's questions and her inability to answer them. When Judy and I read about the Stages of Alzheimer's in the information the doctor provided, we were in agreement that Mom had entered the Sixth Stage of the disease by the time we move her to the Siuslaw Care Center.

Severe cognitive decline
(Moderately severe or mid-stage Alzheimer's disease)

Memory difficulties continue to worsen, significant personality changes may emerge and affected individuals need extensive help with customary daily activities. At this stage, individuals may:

- Lose most awareness of recent experiences and events as well as of their surroundings.

- Recollect their personal history imperfectly, although they generally recall their own name.

- Occasionally forget the name of their spouse or primary caregiver, but generally can distinguish familiar from unfamiliar faces.

- Need help getting dressed properly; without supervision, may make such errors as putting pajamas over daytime cloths or shoes on wrong feet.

- Experience disruptions in their normal sleep/waking cycles.

- Need help with handling details of toileting (flushing toilet, wiping and disposing of tissue properly).

- Have increasing episodes of urinary or fecal incontinence.

- Experience significant personality changes and behavioral symptoms, including suspiciousness and delusions (for example, believing that their caregiver is an imposter); hallucinations (seeing or hearing things that are not really there); or compulsive, repetitive behaviors such as hand wringing or tissue shredding.

- Tend to wander and become lost.

June 28, 2000

Hi James,

You must be both physically and emotionally exhausted. You have been a wonderful son! I don't know that most sons would have taken on this responsibility. This new situation sounds very promising. If Mom is in Florence I can see her more often myself. My phone visit with Mom was good, I think. Her conversation was quite normal. She asked about the boys and who was staying in her house in Yakima. Much better than the last time I talked with her. Take care of yourself. Love you,

Judy

When I walked in she beaded up her eyes and sucked her lips thin like the edge of a clamshell. "This place is worse than all the rest," were her words as she pushed the walker to the side and walked into the bathroom. I stood and waited.

When she was done I pushed her walker in her direction and said, "You will need this Mom." She grabbed it and planted it in front of herself. She then wedged it in her doorway and stripped away some finish as she dropped in tears to her bed. With a kick at the leg of the walker she said, "I want to go home." We talked the you-don't-get-to have-what-you-want talk and I kissed her good-bye. She was crying as I left. I wondered if we would be ending our visits with tears for a while.

June 29, 2000

Hi James,

Thank you for calling. Mom has been on my mind all day. So glad all is looking good. Glad you and Suzanne are able to go back to a normal life, too. Will Mom be able to take personal calls and what about an address and phone numbers?
Thank you, Thank you.

Love, Judy

JULY

July 1, 2000

This morning Mom was sitting by the front door with her purse in hand. She flashed me her angry look and said, "Get me out of here." I laughed and hugged her. We signed out of the care center and walked for a block. She talked about wanting to go home and how long her days feel. "I have been up for hours and hours walking the halls," she said. The walk helped. On the way back she talked about a favored nurse and how good the food was. I told her that Suzanne and I would be back in the afternoon to take her for a drive. She said, "I will like that."

Hi James,

Thanks for keeping me up to date on how Mom is doing. She is on my mind a lot. I talked to Gail last night. I told her Mom could move around pretty much as she pleased and it was OK in this place. Gail said it was the same for her mom until she started getting in bed with the other patients. The staff frowned on that. Gail said it lasted for about a month. Any warm body she could find, she crawled in bed with. So be prepared! It sounds like Mom is doing OK and the Care Center is much better than the residential home. Is she crying or frightened? I have so many questions. Are you exhausted? You are a kind, kind man.

Love, Judy

I took Mom for a drive up the north fork of the Siuslaw River and out to the South Jetty. When I picked her up at the care center, I looked down the hall and saw her talking with two other ladies. She was animated and seemed happy. Her bright sweater and tan slacks reminded me of gone-by days when Mom was running the show and looking good doing it. When she saw me she immediately changed hats to show me the poor-and-left-to-rot woman, who is treated badly by her children. I asked her, "Do you want to go for a ride, Mom?" Her reply was a harsh, "Damn rights! Anything to get out of this prison." Our drive was a mix of look-at-those-beautiful-hills-and-the-cows-by-the-creek, and why-are-you-doing-this-to-me? statements. I personally liked talking about the cows.

We watched the motorbikes and ATV's rush up, down and across the massive sand dune mountains. "I've never seen anything like that in my life," were Mom's words as rig after rig flashed past our front window. When we turned into the care center's driveway, we began an intense why-are-you-doing-this-to-me discussion. It ended with Mom and I doing our verbal tango around her wanting to go home and challenging me with "What right do you have to keep me in this hospital?" All in all it was a three on a scale of ten with ten being a great visit.

Sweet Sister,

I was thinking this afternoon that I was anxious about how you would view my choices in care for Mom. I want you to know that I have done the best I could with what was available to me. Being able to be with and check on Mom is very high on my list, even though she is most often mad at me. My second consideration was the quality of care. The staff is comprised of RNs and LPNs with CNAs doing much of the hard work. They are sweet and gentle with their patients. The building is older, but clean with fresh paint and wallpaper. It looks like a nursing home and is filled with all the folks you would expect. I don't like the idea of Mom being in such a place. However, I know that she would not be happy in the fanciest Alzheimer unit in the world.

She has several friends and views herself as being in a hospital and better off than most of the other patients. Soon, if what everyone tells us is true, she will not be one of the better offs. If, when you come to visit, you feel that it is too much of a nursing home for you and want to move her to another location, I wouldn't be hurt. I would be hurt, though, if I thought you felt that I wasn't caring for Mom as best I could. That is my fear and that is why I am writing you this note.

James

At this point it was time to give the extended family some news of Mom and her condition. So many things had changed since Mom left Yakima just a few short weeks ago. It was hard to know where to begin when explaining all that we had been through and all that we had learned. This letter went out to my aunts, uncles, and cousins.

Dear Family,

I hope this letter finds you all well. I want to tell you about Mom and how she is doing. As you all know Judy and I asked Nan if she would care for Mom following Dad's death. Nan gave it a great effort under very difficult circumstances. Had we known Mom was suffering from Alzheimer's we would have made different decisions. We did know that there were problems and were not surprised when her doctor diagnosed her with the disease. Mom was angry in Yakima and she is angry in Florence.

At this stage of her disease she is anxious, frustrated, disappointed, confused and, most prevalent, angry. Others who have shared their experiences with their Alzheimer's patients have reported that this is common. In time, we are told, she will be more peaceful and content.

If you wish to write to Mom, a nurse will read your letters to her. She will enjoy them in the moment she receives them and forget that you wrote ten minutes later. She will though, enjoy the moment.

Thanks family for all the love we have shared,

James Heintz

Hi Sweet Sister,

Mom had on her beady eyes and stuck out her tongue. She stayed mad for the visit and responded little to my teasing. She wouldn't let us tuck her in. I left her sitting on the edge of her bed with her pink nightgown around her waist.

I wanted to tell you that your plans to visit Florence are great. Suzanne and I will be gone July 14th through the 17th. We are going to Los Angeles to see Jordan, and to attend a wedding. Our home is yours, whether we are there or not.

James

July 2, 2000

Judy and I just talked on the phone. She assured me that she was in support of my care of Mom. We talked and talked. We have a need to be unified on this rolling ball of Mom's life, but find ourselves under it more often than in control of it. I know that this is the best I can do for my mother, and am not yet able to feel that this is the best that I can do.

July 3, 2000

Hi Sweet Sister,

Last night Suzanne and I took Mom out to dinner at a Norwegian restaurant called Café Synnove. Excellent food. We will take you there when you come to visit. Mom was a delight. She did tell one of her hallway friends, "Ya know, they served the same meal at that restaurant that they served in our restaurant." The two old gals then decided to share a walker. Mom took one handle and the other hung her cane on the front, grabbed her side and together, with huge smiles of success, they pushed the walker down the hall wandering from one side to the other, as other hall-walkers smiled. We had a few moments that were difficult, but only a few.

James

Mom was at the door at 8:30 a.m. with purse in hand. "Get me out of here," she said. I hooked her arm in mine, and we walked half a block. She started to lean hard to the right and had a difficult time. She also talked about her feelings being hurt because I had left her and had married another woman. She has started mixing me up with Dad. Getting back to the care center was done with effort. A short little walk was more than she could do today.

Mom was in bed today sporting her bra and panties and was very confused. She was also back to the how-could-I-leave-her-and-marry-another dialog. It was a short visit. After ten minutes I was out the door and away from her.

July 4, 2000

Mom was being lead down the hall for her shower when I arrived this morning. I watched TV for a bit with a handful of patients. She was trying to be happy today and to stay away from subjects that caused her tears and frustrated me. A few minutes into the visit she failed and began to cry about my leaving her for another woman. We never quite got away from her losses from then on. Suzanne and I are having Jamie over for the 4th of July. I have such mixed feelings about bringing Mom home. She would love it. Maybe I will bring her over a little later in the day after we go crabbing.

Jamie arrived around 2:00 p.m. and we spent several hours walking Old Town in the rain. When we got back to the house we all got in the van and drove to the care center. Mom was in her nightie. The CNAs at the Center dressed her up and we were quickly out the door and on our way to dinner. I took videos and we all enjoyed her. During my morning visit I had talked with her about how difficult it was for me to deal with her anger around her thinking I was Dad with another wife. "I'm your son, Mama! Dad died. He didn't leave you. Suzanne is my wife and I'm your son." The talk seemed to help. She put her very best foot forward and we were delighted. After dinner and lots of talk, Mom said that she was tired and wanted to go home. I couldn't believe that she referred to the care center as home, but she did. We took her back and said good night. Smiles were everywhere.

July 5, 2000

She had tears and more tears today. "Get me out of this prison," she cried. Mom knows that her crying is hard for me and tries to change the subject. She wants me to visit and is fearful that if she keeps making the visits difficult I will quit coming. Judy just called, so I am out the door with a kiss. Saved by my sister again. She calls Mom a lot. I hope she gets a good rate on her phone bill.

July 6, 2000

Mom was great today, both in the morning and the evening. She was peaceful and easy in her talk. There was softness in her eyes and she smiled and had ease in my leaving. No negative talk and no tears. The staff seems to love her. Often they stop for a hug from "Tootsie." I think it has some thing to do with her candy habit. I can listen to her talk for twenty minutes and have no idea what she is talking about. Her mind slides from reality to fantasy, from visits with the living and the dead, to exciting adventures and humorous occurrences that couldn't have occurred.

Tonight she escaped from the care center for a few minutes. The staff called me to say that she found an open gate in the garden area and walked around the grounds. When I asked her about it she said, "I didn't hear about that." She did want to tell me about Steve (my dead brother) and what he had to say.

Good Morning James,

Just read your mail. Sure glad to hear Mom was having a better day yesterday. Looking forward to seeing you next week. "Tootsie" that fits Mom! Hope she is moving into a better stage for both of your sakes!

Love you, Judy

Just as I was worrying about and caring for Mom, my kids exchanged concerns about me and how the care of my mother was affecting my own well-being. My daughter was close enough to come for weekend visits, but my son was too far away and had to rely on emails and phone calls to assess my levels of distress about the task at hand. I wrote him the following email in an effort to reassure:

July 7, 2000

My Dear Son Jordan,

Yes it is difficult. I keep thinking that I can transcend the thorny parts and explain it away with the disease. When Mom looks me in the eyes and cries because I have been unfaithful to her, it is not easy. This warmed attitude that I experienced yesterday may have been a one-day thing, but I hope I get to see more of it. Your father, this man of steel, thinks that he can ride the top of the waves and finds himself all too often in the river's muck. Must be the armor.

Mom is in a wheel chair. They said that her legs hurt and that she didn't have much strength in them. I didn't like seeing her sitting there. This afternoon I found Mom in bed. She takes off her cloths and puts on a nightie for afternoon naps. She also often doesn't know whether it is morning or evening.

Today I dropped into her rocking chair and we talked. She lay on her side and smiled often. Her attitude around our visit reminded me of high school girls visiting in an upstairs bedroom. Our time was longer than normal and she told me about her making every bed in the unit. "Oh yes, they make me make the beds everyday. I do a pretty good job too," she said. She also reported having several visits to the doctor today and was disappointed in how little he knew. She went on to say, "And those nurses. They are so bossy. Go here. Go there. Why can't they figure out what they want?"

She is proud today of her personal power. "That preacher that runs the church, well, he tried to tell me what I should believe and I told him a thing or two. I don't think he knew who he was messing with when he tried to push his ideas on me," she said. She huffed and puffed and smiled at her quick thoughts. I loved our visit. I loved her smile.

Dad

July 8, 2000

Saturday morning was a skip and hit visit with Mom. She doesn't like it when it's so short, but says that it is better than nothing. Suzanne and I had a day-trip planned to take three little boys to Wildlife Safari in Winston, Oregon, as a good student reward from Suzanne. We took Mom for a drive up to Mercer Lake after we had returned from our trip. Mom loved the heavy tree growth and the ferns and was delighted when we treated her to ice cream. She had strawberry, but didn't get much eaten before it melted. Melting ice cream has been a life-long problem for her, and is worse now with the Alzheimer's. She laughed and licked as creamy liquid drizzled down her hands.

July 9, 2000

This morning I did another skip and hit. We were having folks over for dinner and I needed to clean and prepare. Around five o'clock, I picked her up and brought her home. She is always on her best behavior when others are around, and she did very well. She smiled a lot and had little to say. When the evening was over she told me, "You can be quite a fancy man when you want to, can't you?" Around eight, she was out of gas and needed to go home. Her leg bothers her a lot. Sciatica is what they are calling it. They have been giving her pain meds for several days to help her with it. She doesn't do well with Tylenol or Ibuprophen. Both make her sick to her stomach. She did have a good appetite, though, and loved the watermelon.

July 10, 2000

Mom greeted me with tears this morning. "You bought the insurance that got me in here. What are you going to do about it? I have been here for days! What do you think you are doing?" Most of her clothes were out of her closet and her little carry bag was full of the pictures and stuff I had put on the corkboard mounted on the wall of her room. All her underwear was missing. She said she gave it all away.

This afternoon I helped Mom into a wheelchair and we rolled through the area neighborhoods. The wind was blowing and took her breath away. Today was also the first day that Mom didn't dress with her typical class. She had on black shoes, one sock, gray slacks, and a pink floral dress. She was also without makeup. We laughed on our walk and admired the yards and houses. She was tired when we got back, so I left her in her room.

Hi James,

We got home from the cabin this morning. We are washing clothes, getting ready for tomorrow and looking forward to seeing you, Suzanne and Mom. How is your weather? Should we pack for both warm and cool weather? Is Mom feeling better about being in her new home? I'll give you a call tonight. Bye for now.

Love, Judy

July 11, 2000

Mom was in a wheelchair this morning. She was a tearful mess and was not able to move away from her tears for most of my visit. I rolled her into the glass dining room and we sat and talked. "I don't understand why you are keeping me in this prison. I haven't done anything so wrong." Her thoughts skipped. She was not able to find any joy in her circumstances.

I just got a call from the care center. Mom fell and banged her head. They don't understand her loss of leg strength this past week, possibly a bladder infection. Judy will be here tonight. I'm glad that she coming.

Between July 11th and the 13,th Judy and her husband, Mag, were in Florence. The visit was wonderful. Judy supported all that I am doing with Mom and felt good about the care center. She and Mag took Mom on drives, out to eat and spent lots of time with her. Judy surveyed Mom's wardrobe, replacing the missing underwear and adding some easy-to-put-on items. Mom loved it. I loved it.

July 18, 2000

Hi James,

We had a very nice visit and enjoyed Florence. Thank you again. Our trip home went well. Hope you and Suzanne had a great weekend. I called Mom Saturday and she was OK. She had been taken outside and was very pleased about it. Sunday I called and she was very sad. We talked for about twenty-five minutes. I reassured her that Dad did not divorce her. It seemed to help at the time. This morning I called her and she was OK again. She had been singing and had enjoyed it. She remembered Mag and our visiting her. The conversations were pretty good. Of course there were the regular diversions. She said that she would like a little money to go shopping and that she would like Katharine to give her a call. My little update!

Lots of Love, Judy

I have been gone for four days on a trip to L.A. to see my son, Jordan, and returned to a new regression in Mom's mental processing. I was so concerned that she would be upset with my absence. Feeling appreciable anxiety when I first saw her in the hall, I called her name. She turned and greeted me as if I hadn't been gone. With a smile on her face, like a girl with a new boy friend, Mom introduces me to the old ladies in the hall. "This is my husband." We talked for a few minutes and then she began her conversation, "I don't know what I did wrong. Why I drove you off. Why you married that other woman." Her tears were heavy and she wanted me to hold her. Her hug wasn't a Mom hugging her son. It was my mother hugging my father. As hard as I try to appreciate the Alzheimer and Mom's inability to manage her processing, I feel caught up in sexual improprieties. I became frustrated as I, for the hundredth time, talked about my marriage, my wife and Mom's knowing about and supporting it all. No matter how I say it, no matter how many times I say it, it doesn't change. I am her husband and have left her for another woman and she is devastated. She rubs my arm and slides her hand up my sleeve and rubs my shoulder. Mama, Mama!!!

Sweet Sister,

This afternoon I was working on a house owned by the local funeral company and decided to take a little time to find about Mom's future death and how I would get her body home to Yakima and what laws would be involved in the process. I was pleased to discover that there are few problems involved and it can be inexpensive. I will find out more this afternoon.

I love you Sister, James

July 19, 2000

Mom is much the same today. She said to me this morning as I was leaving because she was back on the how-could-you-do-this-to-me dialog, "Why don't you kiss me on the lips and see what happens?" Ick!!! This is hard.

July 20, 2000

I saw Mom twice today. She tried real hard not to talk about my being her husband and her being so hurt that I had left her for another. She did well until the end of our visit tonight. It was OK.

July 21, 2000

"This is a prison, get me out of here," has become the common tearful greeting. I laugh, hug and then we walk to the patio where we visit. Today she reported that she was being treated badly. "They think I am a rebel. It's just a few things that I have said, ya know, at the dinner place. I told them too much and now they, even the ones that like me, are looking at me and watching. I played the piano for them. Did a pretty good job, too. Oh ya, they think I am Miss Twinkle Fingers." I checked with the staff and sure enough Mom has become the Queen of the Ivories. She has played for them several times and loves the attention. She said that she has sung along on a song or two. I love it.

July 22, 2000

It's Saturday, so Mom and I took a long drive up Highway 101. She loved the sights. She talked to me all the way. Despite my requests for her to speak more loudly, she didn't and I missed most of what she was sharing. She cried a lot when I returned her to the care center.

July 23, 2000

Sunday I decided that I needed a day off and wouldn't visit. I so often feel bad after our visits that I needed the break. I spent the day doing normal things … cleaning the garage, mowing the lawn, cleaning the dog run, washing the car … with little thought of Mom or Alzheimer's. I got a call late Sunday afternoon from Jordan in California. Mom had called and told him that she was in jail in Yakima. She wanted him to hunt me down and get her out. Jordan called me and I went over to visit her and her tears.

July 24, 2000

This morning she was, as I often find her, standing by the nurses' station with her purse in her hand. Her tears were quick. We walked outside onto the patio and sat. She cried, we talked, and when it was time for me to leave, she expected me to take her home. Then she surprised me by asking about the care center. She said that she had never been inside and was interested about it. When we walked in she delighted in the tile floor that she has been walking on for a month. "Isn't it beautiful? Did you do this yourself?" she asked. When I told her that this was lovely place was her home and I wouldn't be taking her with me when I left, she cried.

Hi James,

I talked to Mom on the phone today. She was very confused. The nurse said she had a bad day yesterday. Katharine called me today and was concerned about Mom too. She had called and found her to be in pretty bad shape, confused. The way Mom talked we wondered if something actually had happened. She was so upset about being locked in and being constrained in bed. Do you know anything about this or is Mom having a really bad time right now with her confusion? Today Mom's confusion was different.

Love Judy

Sweet Sister,

Mom has been very confused. She walks out of the building into the garden area, looks back and asks, "What is this place? Have I been here before? She doesn't remember your being here. I had not heard about Katharine's call until your email. She doesn't know morning from late afternoon. She is totally confused about where she lives and eats. All she seems to have a handle on is the moment and that is hard because her moment is filled with feelings of being confined, over-powered and without choice. She is also talking a lot about moving to her little house on Tieton Drive. She thinks that she would be OK there. I asked her this morning about Dad. She didn't know who I was talking about. "Mom, tell me about Dad, tell me about Johnny." Her response was, "I don't know a Johnny and I haven't seen my Dad for a long time. Do you know where he is?" She is not having much fun with her life lately. I will keep you posted.

James

Some dear friends, Tom and Victoria Schneider, came to dinner tonight. Tom said that his dad died of Alzheimer's. I think he was concerned about the amount of time I was spending with Mom and the negative effect those visits were having on me. He warned me about getting engulfed by the process. He said that he had employed great effort in protecting himself from his father's disease.

After the Schneiders left I found myself thinking about Judy's call and I, at 10:07 in the evening, drove over to the care center to check on Mom. I appreciated Tom's counsel and probably won't follow his advice.

July 25, 2000

Mom was in pretty good spirits today. Both this morning and this evening she was calm and sweet when I greeted her, and was only a little difficult when I left. Tonight she couldn't understand why I wouldn't take a few minutes to drive her by her house. "I don't have any other way to get home, if you don't take me," she said. She had received a letter from Katharine, which I read to her. She didn't remember Judy's or Katharine's phone calls from yesterday.

Hi James,

Glad to hear Mom is doing a little better. How was she able to call Jordan? Did the staff help her? Also Katharine wondered if she was sharing a room now. Mom told her that she was. Take care of yourself!!!

Love you, Judy

July 26, 2000

She was sitting in the lobby with all the other folks this morning. She is never with the other folks. I always find her alone or maybe with one other patient. When she saw me she jumped up. Well, she didn't jump up, but her eyes jumped.

She is working very hard at not crying when I visit and did a good job today with several close-to-tears calls, which she was able to avoid. When I left she didn't ask to come along and smiled as she waived good-by. She has developed a new interest in the buildings behind the care center and enjoys talking about their roofs, fences, siding and windows. We also discuss the colors they are painted. One of the staff said that Mom dresses so well that she is often viewed as a visitor by other visitors. Mom would like that.

July 27, 2000

Not a great visit. I didn't get by this morning due to getting up late and having lots of work to do. This afternoon Mom greeted me with tears. We walked out to the garden area and sat down. She cried about having no calls, no visits, and no family that cared. She wanted to go home. I tried to talk around these issues and when she began to harp on the, "Oh, you have your own family. I can't believe that you left me for her. I didn't even know that we were divorced." I became angry. Not huff and puff anger, just "God Mom, cut me some slack. I'm your kid not your husband. You liked my wife and supported our marriage. I didn't sneak off and do something bad. I just want to come here and visit you and talk about the sky, flowers and the houses across the street." Her reply was to get up and walk, without her walker, away from me. She got half way down the path and stopped. A nurse from inside came out with Mom's walker and said, "Mr. Heintz, if you are going to be with your mother you need to be beside her." Damn! Bad again. Mom came back and informed me, "I want to go home. Will you drive me?" I said, "Oh Mom, you live here and home is nine hours away in Yakima." We went back and forth. Finally I got up and walked her in to dinner. When I kissed her and began to leave she got to her feet. "You aren't going to leave me here. I am going with you." It took another five minutes to leave and her parting words were, "I will never forgive you for this. I will never forgive you for leaving me." Only one word whispered across my lips, "Shit!"

I attended my first Alzheimer's support group late this afternoon. It was sad to listen to the husbands and wives that are living with this disease day in and day out. It's killing me and I am only dealing with it an hour or two a day with lots of breaks.

July 28, 2000

I spent time with Mom this morning and took her to the doctor in the afternoon. I think yesterday was hard on her spirit. I feel bad. One of the staff RN's said that she over heard my frustrations with Mom and gave me advice. "She will not respond to logic," she said. "Just soothe her and let her confusion pass by you." It was very good advice. Today she just said, "Talk to me about happy things." So we talked and talked about old times and the kids and their lives. She seemed to like the visits. So did I.

The doctor's visit seemed like a waste of time. Although he treats us very well while I share my concerns about her depression and health, I listen between the lines of his words and hear, "She is an old woman with Alzheimer's ... what do you expect?" He did order a psychological evaluation.

Hi James,

The kids went water skiing this morning. If you want good water, you have to get out on the lake early in the morning. The lake gets pretty busy on the weekends. Bryan and Karrie are going home tomorrow. It has been nice having them here this week. I care and am interested in the blow-by-blow happenings with Mom. I feel so sorry for both you and Mom. Was the doctor able to help Mom in any way? I would think she would be exhausted from all the tears. Has the support group been of any help? We are going into the Bay Area on Monday. Mag's cousin is having her ninetieth birthday. Her mind is pretty sharp. Life definitely isn't fair. However, for many years she has not wanted to be alive any longer. This aging process is not so easy, is it?

Judy

July 29, 2000

"Would you like to go for a drive Mom?" "Damn rights!" was her reply. The staff said that she was very wobbly on her feet today and they had her in a wheel chair. I signed her out and Suzanne and I rolled her to the van. "Oh, thank you for taking me out. I come close to going stir crazy when I don't get away from this place." We drove for three hours and went deep into the coastal woods and around part of Lake Siltcoos. The road we chose ended at a resort called Ada. The last nine miles of the road was one lane and passing a car going in the opposite direction would have been difficult. The view was scrumptious. Trees, ferns, under growth, blue skies, lakes, rivers, bridges, birds and deer were splashed across our windows and filled our van with delight. Mom was happy and talked like a magpie. Much of what she said was too soft to hear or composed in incomplete sentences, which could start on a deer and end on the color of Suzanne's socks. It didn't matter today. Mom was happy.

July 30, 2000

This mid-morning she was sitting out in the lobby on the love seat alone. The room was full of people and Mom had shoved her walker over and was slumped across the entire seat and tearful. Within moments of my sitting with her, she was smiling and talking. She told me about her singing in the choir and how pleased she is with her voice. "They think quite a lot of me, you know. I do have a good voice, and they have noticed." She also talked about the youth yelling outside her Tieton Drive house and her going out to look at them. We talked about the new ninth grade class she will be teaching and my two wives. She goes on and on. I timed my visit forty-five minutes before lunch so I would have a smooth departure. I liked the visit.

I have spent my adult life feeling that everyone, including myself, is better off looking at the reality of life and dealing with it. Mom does not benefit from reality. She can't change anything. She lives in another world that I cannot change. So, whatever you say, Mom, "IS," and I am in full support of everything you believe and say.

The staff informed me that last week the psychologist from Eugene came and visited with Mom. She stated that if she prescribed meds for Mom's anxiety they would make her much more prone to falling. She also felt that Mom is in a grieving process and she, because of the Alzheimer's, is not grieving in a traditional way. She also felt that allowing Mom to grieve was the path to follow at this time.

Hello James,

Bryan and Karrie just left. The house is so quiet now. We really enjoyed their visit. Adult children are fun aren't they! I was glad to know that Mom had an evaluation. I keep forgetting that Mom lost Dad only four months ago. What you said makes sense. In the big picture it would be best that Mom keep walking. Hopefully, in time the sadness will become less. Confusion is OK but I sure hope the tears and sadness are not a permanent condition.

As for the house, I agree that we will need to take care of the contents. I have a hard time with the idea of distributing Mom's property while she is alive, but know that is what needs to be done. I am sure there are some things that you would like and there are some things that I would like to have. What do you think? I think I need to take a nap. I can't keep up with these kids any more. They remind me of my age. Bye for now.

Love, Judy

July 31, 2000

I caught Mom in her room this morning. She was washing up. She had on the gray slacks that she had spilled Popsicle juice on Saturday. I mentioned the stain and she responded with a, "Nobody else cares, why should I?" She also said, "I'm slipping. I can feel it. I can't even remember how to get to where we eat."

The staff has noticed that she is back to walking with a tilt to the left. It looks like her balance is off and standing is difficult. They wanted me to keep a hand on her when she's moving with her walker to avoid a fall.

The staff seems to keep a closer eye on Mom than some of the other patients. Maybe it's because she has enough of her oars in the water to be interesting. She continues to be the Florence Nightingale of the ward and can't pass another patient without a pat or a word of support. She was full of chatter today and is sweet.

She again talked about the compliments she has received for her beautiful singing voice. Boasting about her good voice gives her pleasure. There were a few complete thoughts today and she again asked why the family wasn't sending her cards. I understand why and yet I am afraid that Mom is out-of-sight, out-of-mind for lots of the family. I am going to mail out another request for cards.

Dear Aunt Katharine,

I have enclosed a lot of the e-mail that Judy and I have exchanged. It will give you a feeling of how Mom is doing. She is not happy and wouldn't be happy any where. She does have moments when her life seems OK. We try to make as many of those moments happen as we can.

Tell the family that cards are good for Mom. When she feels alone I point to your letters and cards that are on her pegboard and it helps.

Mom often talks about you and loves you so,

James

AUGUST

August 1, 2000

I was able to visit twice with Mom today. This morning she had many stories to tell me and talked about all her little visits to her home. Today, when she was over there, she cleaned the place up a bit. It has been a while and she was surprised how much dust had collected. We also talked about her anger around being locked up. "Why, I will tell you James, they watch me. They are watching me all the time. I don't know how they found out about my house, but they are bound and determined to keep me from going over there. Now do you think that is right? And who gave them the power to tell me what I can and can't do?" "Don't you worry about it Mom. I will talk to them and share your concerns," I said.

This afternoon she met me at the door as if we were going to bust out. "Come on!! Don't sit down!! We have got to get out of here!!" "Hold on Mom," I said, "what's happening?" "I gotta get out of this place now. They have got all the doors locked and the only way I am going to get out of here is with you," she said. We sat and talked. I could see the wind blow from her sails as I told her that I couldn't bust her out. I had to go to a meeting. "Just get me out the door. I can walk to my house from here. It's not that far. I did it this afternoon." I walked her to her room and from there to dinner. I gave her a kiss and promised to see her tomorrow morning. She gave me that you-are-not-a-knight-in-shining-armor look and kissed me good-by.

August 3, 2000

Mom was really angry at the world and at some preacher that had visited the care center. I took her for a drive. We sat at the edge of the beach in my truck and watched the waves roll in, hoping to soak in some of its peace. We said a couple of prayers, drove around for a while and then we went back.

Hi James,

I talked to Mom this morning. Actually, she talked for about forty-five minutes. I tell you this because she had very nice things to say about you and your caring about her. She does appreciate the time you give her very much. She told me about her fall and her fight with the preacher. She did say she pooped on the floor. I am not sure about that one! I will start sending her mail now too. Like I said, I have been calling her about every three days. I hope she doesn't think I put her on the back burner. Also, today she told me how she thought you were her husband for a while. She felt bad about that. Will talk to you soon.

Love, Judy

August 4, 2000

I didn't see Mom today. Judy called. We talked about her.

August 5, 2000

I received a wonderful gift from God this morning when I visited with Mom. She was clear in her thoughts and we talked about several subjects that were important. I asked her about her view of God. She said, "I get mad at preacher types because they try to judge and force upon me their view of God and how I am to live my life. I have loved God all my life. I was taught as a child about God and I fully accepted it all." We talked about death. She told me, "I don't know what happens. I believe that something will happen, and I don't know what it is. I do know that it will be what God wants and that is good enough for me." Mom talked a lot about Dad and his death. "He was a good man and was loved by many people. He wasn't a perfect man. Other than his drinking, he was a great fellow." She cried and said, "I feel so alone without him. Being with family is so important. Most people don't know how important family is."

Steve was next on the agenda and she said, "Steve was never happy. He didn't think life was going to give him a fair shake and made sure it didn't. I wasn't surprised when he took his life. John and I figured that it could happen some day." Mom also told me that she appreciated me and she was glad that I visited her.

August 6, 2000

"My son is here to visit now," was what Mom told my sister Judy, who had been talking with her on the phone, when I arrived. The staff nurse quickly caught my attention and shared, "She's real unstable on her feet today. Be careful." After saying "Hi" to Judy on the phone, I hung up and helped Mom to her feet. She began with, "Some of the old battle axes around here don't like me. Let's go outside where we can talk." Mom's balance was poor. She was close to falling several times. Once seated in the plastic patio chairs she said, "I am slowly losing the battle. Every morning I feel weaker." We talked for an hour. I finished our visit by saying, "I am going to go crabbing when I leave. I would take you with me, but I'm pretty sure you would end up being fish food." She replied with an, "I'm not too sure that wouldn't be OK."

Though I often felt very alone in my struggles with Mom, family members continued to toss me lines of support. Here is a letter from Aunt Katharine.

August 7, 2000

Dear James & Suzanne,

Thanks so much for sending the E-mail. It helps to read about her progress. My heart goes out to you both. It is so hard to go through this illness with someone you care so much about. Keith's mom thought Warren (his brother) was her husband. He was fortunate not to be around too much. It must be the most frustrating thing in the world on how to handle it. You feel sorry for them, a little hurt and a little angry because it is such an awkward position to be in. James, your friend was right, you can't let this consume your life and thoughts. It will if you aren't careful. I know your Mom, nor your Dad, would what that to happen. You are doing a loving, wonderful act of kindness to your Mom. She knows it. She is just hating herself, her situation and the world, not you kids. We all have tried our best. There is no answer. Don't let it eat you up. I know that it is hard not too. I have to remind myself that all I can do is pray for her, write and phone her and let her know we care. I have cried when I opened the glove compartment and out fell her suckers. I cried when the car got dust on it. I have grieved for your Mom more than for your Dad, but because I felt he is at peace. Your Mom is in a hell right now that we can't be at peace with. It is probably hurting all of us more sometimes than it is her. It is a gut-wrenching thing to go through and seems so unfair. It is not something you can walk away from. She is getting a lot of love and care from the people that love her and at least that sinks through part of the time. You are a wonderful, devoted, son. Thank you for such good care of my big sister. I called her today. She talked just as sensible and clear for five minutes then wham! She was talking about your Dad selling all his properties (six houses) and not letting her know and went on and on. She also then said about having Alzheimer's and how she got things mixed up and couldn't remember and how scary it was. Just pray she gets past this stage pretty fast and even if it kills us for her not to know us it would, I hope, be better for her. Just feel good that you kids are doing your best.

Love, Aunt Katharine

August 7, 2000

It was mid-day when I visited Mom. She was sitting on the patio with one of the CAN's. They know how important it is for Mom to get out, so they assign someone to her and let them sit or wander around the grounds for a while. I am pleased about that consideration. Mom was quick to drop her brow and give me her I-am-mad-at-the-world look. I held her hand and laughed. "Tell me about it, Mom. Who is on your shit list today?" Mom scrunched her eyes down closer to her lips and said, "The preacher and that young fool that runs this place. They both go running when I come around the corner." "Wow Mom, tell me more," I said. She did and that is how we spent most of our visit. We went back to her room before I left and looked for her watch and Tootsie Pops which have both disappeared this week. She probably gave them away or tossed them in the garbage.

Hi James,
What a nice and supportive letter Kathryn wrote you. Does she do e-mail? Do they have a computer? It would be nice to e-mail her too. Glad to hear that Mom is getting outside regularly. Are you still able to take her for walks?

Love, Judy

August 9, 2000

"Hi, Mom. I just have a minute. Judy called and said that you were having a terrible day. Are ya?" She said, "Ya dam rights I am! Wouldn't you go crazy if you were kept a prisoner?" I told her that I couldn't stay and that I would be back late in the afternoon to take her to dinner at our house. She responded with, "Good! I'll look forward to that." I dashed out the door and did my day's work.

When I spotted her down the hall around 4:00 p.m. she almost ran to me. "Do you want to come over to my house for dinner, Mom?" I asked. She didn't even pause to talk. She grabbed my arm and towards the door we went. She didn't even ask about her purse. That's a change. Once in the car she began to talk. Mom spent the next three hours talking about what she was seeing and enjoying herself greatly. We sat on the backyard swing and watched the dogs. I got out the photo album and showed her pictures of her house in Yakima and the last photographs of Dad, she cried. We walked in the yard and admired the flowers. When it began to cool we went inside and she sat at the kitchen table while I prepared dinner. Suzanne was late getting home from work, so we ate alone. We had a big salad and ice cream. Mom's mind was working very well. It made me wonder why I had her living in a locked care unit. She wasn't unwilling to go home, but when I drove up to the care center she began to cry. "I thought you were taking me home," she said. I immediately felt a lump in my throat the size of an apple. "I'm sorry, Mom. Home is too far away."

August 10, 2000

"Well now. Aren't we curly?" was my greeting when I spotted Mom coming down the hall with her new perm. She was being escorted to the phone to talk with her grandson, Bryan. I sat there and watched her eyes glitter as they visited. She smiled and leaned back in her chair and crossed her legs on her walker like a company executive having a conference call. When she hung up the phone she said, "He is such a good boy. He has done so much for John and I. I like it that he is watching out for me." We walked out to the garden and sat in the plastic chairs. We talked about all the things in Mom's mind that aren't real. The buildings we own, her home up the street and my taking her there after our visit. She said that she had received cards in the mail and she had. Katharine has sent her both a letter and card. The little sister loves the big sister. I had one last project to complete and kissed Mom goodbye. She was OK with my going. I promised that I would return.

Hi James,

Glad to hear Mom had a good evening. I suppose she will never be comfortable going back to the Care Center. Does every outing will have a difficult ending? Do you ever get used to it? I have a few questions. Did Mom ever find her watch? How did her perm turn out? She likes to have curls in her hair. How are the wedding plans going? Is Jamie enjoying this time? That is it for now.

Love, Judy

Two more questions. Are you going to the Alzheimer's support group? If so, is it of any help? Have you or do you think it would be possible or a good idea to get some sense of what Mom feels about selling and removing her furniture etc. It would sure make it easier for us emotionally to make a decision if we felt she approved. Is this wishful thinking on my part?

Judy

Good Morning James,

So Curly is looking curly! Is that good? Was Mom pleased with her new do? Did she say she would like to have a TV in her room? Bryan said that Mom appreciated all the time you give her very much. She does know that you are being very good to her. Bye for now.

Love, Judy

August 11, 2000

Sweet Sister,

I talked with Mom this morning about our selling her stuff. She said, "I don't want you to sell the piano. I will want it when I move. All the rest of the stuff is replaceable." She went on to say, "What I want is a little house with good neighbors who like to talk. That old house is too big. It would be too hard for me to keep clean." Judy, you need to appreciate that she is loosely attached to this subject and she doesn't know where she is now, let alone where she will be tomorrow. I told her we would store lots of her stuff with family so that she could get it back when, and if, she gets better from her Alzheimer's and can get a place of her own. Although she often talks about getting worse both physically and mentally she likes to hold out the hope that some day she will beat this illness and live a normal life. She did say that she didn't think she would marry again.

The staff continues to talk about Mom as being in that hostile/combative mode. She talks about her battles, but I see mostly smiles and whining about having to live with all these nuts. I'm not sure if she is referring to the staff or the patients. She does have an interest in a TV. Maybe I will bring her the one from Yakima. Do you think it is too big? She said that she didn't want us to spend any money on a new one.

She looks like a poodle. She is getting lots of compliments, and it is a kick to watch her do her coy, "Oh gosh, do you really like it?"

Aunt Katharine called last night to support me. She said all the things again that she said in her letter. She thinks that we are good kids and are doing the best that we can do.

James

August 12, 2000

Today we took a trip to Eugene and had coffee with my daughter, Jamie. We then attended a church service where Suzanne's niece preached. After that, I bought a new suit for Jamie's wedding. It was close to mid-afternoon when we got back to Florence and picked Mom up. As expected, she was very pleased to go for a little drive. We started with a slow cruise through several new beachside residential developments. Mom always loves the houses. We stopped at a turn-around beside the beach and watched the people playing, and we talked about feeling old. A spark of adventure flashed across my mind and I, with Suzanne's help, unloaded Mom and headed for the surf. We walked through the soft, warm sand that filled her shoes. She was delighted when we stopped at the packed and damp mid-beach sand and slipped off her shoes and rolled up her dress slacks. "Oh, no! What are you two going to do?" We walked her, one on each arm, across the wet sand and into the surf. I said, "This will make you feel young, Mom." She replied with, "Don't let me fall!" and "That's far enough!" We respected her fears and returned her to dry land, with sand between her toes. Even though the walk back across the sand and up to the car was difficult, Mom kept a big smile across her face. She said, "Now I will have a good story to tell." When we pulled up to the care center she said, "You know, you don't have my approval to keep me here." She was upset with my being married to Suzanne. It was the only sharp statement of the outing. She was greeted at the door by her favorite aide, and quickly began to tell of her beach adventure.

August 13, 2000

"It's Stephen that got me in all this trouble. He talked to the insurance man and I have been on eight months of confinement because of him and your part of it too. It's not all Steve's fault. Now don't you tell him what happened. It will hurt his feelings. Well I guess it doesn't matter, he's dead."

Mom was on a roll tonight. We brought her a new TV. It works well on OPB and one other station. She said it would keep her from feeling lonely at night. "I think I need to get me another man," she said. Why she needed another man, she didn't tell me.

Other than remembering that Steve was dead I spent most of our visit listening to Mom talk on and on about the bad, but very good looking, preacher man who continues to push his religion down her throat and the insurance company that had kept her confined for over eight months. She also reported that the preacher had locked her in the school for two weeks because she stood up to him. She said it was worth it. She had lots of smiles, was very animated, talked loudly and enjoyed knowing that she was standing up for herself, even if she was being punished.

August 14, 2000

Sweet Sister,

I found Mom early this morning walking towards me in the hall. She had on a teal cotton blouse with a sweater patterned in teal, maroon and blue tied around her neck. Her slacks were gray with black loafer shoes. With her new perm, she was a class act. She snapped my broad red suspenders and said, "Aren't you a cutie!" I responded with, "I pale in the presence of such a classy lady." She punched me in the side, and we walked outside. She talked houses today. I asked her thirty do-you-remember-this-or-that-questions about the last house she owned in Yakima and other chit chat items. She couldn't remember anything about it. She did remember the colors she likes and the type of wallpaper she would like to put in a new house. Not too big of a house, though. Just something that she could manage and fix up a bit. She didn't expect much. Towards the end of the visit she began to complain about being locked up and the damn preacher.

I have business coming at me like crazy this week. I love it. I look forward to seeing you in Yakima, Judy. Is Mag coming with you? I was thinking of leaving for Yakima Monday morning. How about you?

James

Hi James,

We will be in Yakima Monday as well. I am not sure what day we will be driving up, but we will be there by Monday. Mag will be there too. I have a few questions about Mom. Did she ever receive the pictures I sent? She says, "No." I sent them priority over a week ago. Did she receive Greg's letter? How is the TV working out? What all do you hope to get done while we are in Yakima? Bye for now.

Love, Judy

Hi Judy,

Mom did get your pictures and Greg's letter today. I read your card to her and we looked at the pictures. The family looks great. She enjoyed Greg's letter, "He is such a good boy," were her words. I have been putting cards up on her wall, and will now add the pictures.

I thought we would clean out the house and all the personal items. Where it will all go? I don't know. I wasn't thinking about painting or anything like that, but it may be necessary. Let's put an ad in the paper for a garage sale. We could reduce a lot of bulk.

I loves you, James

Mom doesn't feel too good this morning. She said she didn't watch TV. I turned it on this morning so she could have noise in her room. It makes it feel a little more home-like.

August 17, 2000

A mid-morning visit today. Mom was on her bed taking a nap. She had her quilt over her and was peacefully resting. She heard me moving in the room and said, "Hi, there, working man." I was painting today and had on clothing that was more paint than fabric. Our visit was short. She didn't remember anything about our having her over for dinner last night. It was a nice evening and Mom visited the gardens and house like she was seeing it all for the first time. She loves our place and often says, "If your Dad could see this place he would really like it. He would be proud of you, James."

August 18, 2000

I spent a lovely day with Suzanne at her new school in Waldport. We delivered a sofa, some new pictures and stuff to make the classroom hers. On the way back into town we popped in on Mom. She gave us the don't-you-ever-do-that-to-me-again look. "How could you leave me for days and days?" she said. I made a mistake yesterday when I visited with her and talked about my going to Yakima to deal with her and Dad's personal property. She did a short circuit and came up with a he-has-abandoned-me-again attitude. Most of our talking was around how lonesome she is, how she has no friends, and how did she ever let me talk her into moving to the care center. I had to take a few Tums after our visit.

Monday Judy and I will travel from our homes, hers in Sacramento, and mine in Florence, to meet in Yakima. The purpose of our trip is to empty our parents' home. Judy and I agree that this is not a pleasure trip. It is a trip to hell and it is the closing of a most important chapter in our lives. We are saying goodbye to the last residence of our parents.

Today I talked to Mom about my being gone for a few days. She said that she felt trapped and alone. She cried. As hard as I try to transcend these moments with Mom, I fail. It is as if she is pulling her blouse open to show me the gaping wound her life has left her and I, I stand there looking at her, while I try to whistle some damned Walt Disney tune.

Judy and I will do OK next week. We weren't very close as children growing up in our parents home, but I have grown to deeply love the impressive woman my sister is. Good things do come from great tests.

August 26, 2000

I spent last week in Yakima attending to Mom's house with my sister Judy. We have decided that Mom won't be returning to Yakima. Her disease has progressed and her need for care has increased and not diminished.

Entering a house that had been filled with all the material possessions of my parents and smelling the dusty odor that comes to a house unoccupied for three months, did not settle well with me. It felt somewhat like a tomb and was not inviting. Judy and I spent three days giving away, keeping and selling the contents of that now empty house. We didn't like it. We didn't like it at all. We agreed that it felt like the closing of a book that we, with child-like expectations, had wanted to stay open forever. I brought Mom's piano home and a couple of her chairs that reminded me of her and her good taste.

Today when I picked her up for our Sunday drive, I was anxious to see how she would behave when she saw her stuff in my house. We had talked about it several weeks ago, but I knew that it would be new today.

August 27, 2000

The care center had called again and said, "Your Mom has fallen. She seems OK. We are watching to see if she has a concussion from hitting her head." She didn't look well when I entered her room. Her hair was wild and she was attempting to pull herself up and out of the wheel chair they had her using. She was pulling on her bed's blankets and having little success. "Hi, Mom. Can I help you?" She replied with, "Yes. Help me get up on my bed. It's too hard for me to pull myself up from this chair." The staff was guessing along with me as to why Mom suddenly took to falling. She has another bladder infection and has been on meds for four days. Maybe that is part of it. We all agree that she can't walk, even with her walker. I can't help but wonder if we haven't passed another permanent step in Mom's deterioration.

We drove around a couple of near by lakes and her spirits lifted. Several times she said, "Oh, thank God you rescued me today. I am so happy to be out of that place." After our little drive we went to my home. She was pleased to see her piano and let me roll her up to it and lock the wheels. She played with the keys for a bit and said, "My hands are stiff. I will play in a while." As she looked around she spotted the chairs and end table that had been in her home. At first she had a reaction of, "Hey, what are you doing with my stuff?" She quickly switched to it being OK, and she was glad that the piano was close by.

We visited for several hours. She was not able to complete a single thought or sentence. She was very verbal and was confused as she jumped from subject to subject. She talked about Dad's current decisions, which she didn't like, then would later acknowledge that he was dead. She said, "Now James, you are the only one left alive, aren't you?" "No, Mom, Judy, Katharine, Keith, Inga and lots of other family members are still alive." "Oh, that's right."

Her over-all spirit was good and we enjoyed each other today. As I drove up to the care center's door she said, "Do I have to stay here?" "Yes," I said, "you need them to help you." Her reply was a soft, "OK."

August 28, 2000

I had wanted to spot Mom walking the halls but found her in her bed. "Hi Mom. I see you had breakfast in bed this morning." She looked in my direction. See seems to be losing weight. There is slackness to her skin and hollowness around her eyes. The same look you see on old, Persian women. She said, "Hi honey. Have you been busy today?" I walked around her bed and moved her glider so I could sit and talk. The chair had been on the other side of her bed between her and the bathroom. The staff and I agree that this chair had played a major roll in Mom's falls. She and the chair would always end up together on the floor. I moved it to the other side of the room.

"I think I'm slipping James. I feel half alive," were her words. There were no jokes this morning. "You feel like your time is getting short Mom?" was my question. Her answer was "Yes." I asked, "are you afraid?" She said, "Yes." I said, "What do you think is going to happen when you die?" She gave me her oh, I-don't-wanna-talk-about-this look and said, "I don't know. I have never known. That is what scares me." I looked at her and her expression of fearful anticipation.

Lots of time seemed to pass. "Mom, do you want to hear what I think?" She said "OK." I leaned forward in my chair to be a little closer to her. Getting Mom to talk about the big stuff was never easy. I shared with her what I believed happened to us when we died and how all the people she loved would be waiting for her. I probably talked too much and when I finished Mom looked at me for a long time with steady and searching eyes. "You think so?" she said. "Ya Mom, I think so." In the afternoon I brought her a pot of flowers.

August 29, 2000

I received the same phone call twice today. The first came at 10:30 a.m. "Mr. Heintz? This is the Siuslaw Care Center. Your mother has fallen." She was sitting in the social area in a wheel chair. "Look what I've done now." She raised her elbow and displayed a half dozen butterfly bandages covering a skin flap as large as a silver dollar. "I don't know how I did it, but I did," she said. I rolled her out to the patio and we talked about her fall and her not understanding why she has lost her balance. She was also amazed in her skin's transparency and slackness on her arms. "It seems like it all is happening at once. I can't stand up and I am losing weight." I teased her about her elephant skin, admired the gladiolas and kissed her goodbye. "I will come by later, Mom." "Good!" was her reply.

The phone rang at 5:00 p.m. and the message was repeated. "We are having her transported to the hospital. She banged her head again and is vomiting." I told the nurse that I would meet the ambulance at the hospital. When Mom arrived I could see that she was frightened. "Hi, girl. Nice rig for an afternoon ride." She smiled at the sight of me. "Oh, I am glad your here." She had vomit on her shirt and was blanched. They quickly took her into X-ray and then drew blood for a full screen. We spent several hours with her nauseated, and my sitting and holding her hand. We joked with the staff and kept our spirits up. "I don't understand why I keep falling. I think I will just lay on the floor and avoid the falls." "Good joke, Mom!" was my reply.

When all was said and done I walked away from the hospital with Mom in a wheel chair, and knowing that she has had several strokes and that she has lots of brain atrophy. I have felt accepting of Mom's Alzheimer's and yet today I felt as if Mom's days were not going to be many. I dislike that feeling.

I cried at dinner when I told my wife about the day and my fears that my days with Mom were numbered. They just called again, "Your Mom is continuing to vomit and we are moving her to room twelve which is closer to the nursing station." "Thanks for the call," was my reply.

August 30, 2000

Two visits with Mom today. They are connecting a personal alarm to her when she is in bed. If she tries to get up on her own, it will go off and the staff will rush to help her. They would like her to use the call button, but she doesn't. Her new room is much closer to the entrance and she will have a roommate. I think that she will enjoy the increased action. She was pretty far from the rest of the population in the other wing. All this change will hopefully help her avoid falling. Both the head of nurses and the administrator talked with me about Mom's progression in her disease. They are in agreement that she is deteriorating very rapidly. Rarely have they seen this. It is normal for the Alzheimer's to take years to strip the victim of mental and physical control. Mom seems to be an exception. Statistics indicate that the average is nine years from diagnosis to death.

August 31, 2000

Judy phoned Tuesday and Wednesday nights. She, like me, is upset with Mom's failing health. Maybe Mom is just having a difficult period of time and will slow in her deterioration. We are unsure what we want for her. Her day-to-day living is far from wonderful. She isn't angry any more and she smiles easily. Acceptance is in place, yet she shook her fist at me when I met her at the hospital the other day. Lately when she eats with her spoon she is on a hunt and peck mission for her mouth. Her eyes seem extra bright, clear, and they sit easy behind her lids. I don't like the idea that they will permanently close some day.

"I am sick and they won't let me be." Mom wasn't happy that the staff had gotten her up for breakfast. She had a yellow tray on her lap to catch the overflow of her meal. They are putting Mom in the can't-eat-on-their-own-or-won't din-ing room. It seems she has had it with food. At dinner she turned to the CNA that feeds her and said, "I don't like you, and you are not going to get me to eat like you did this morning." "Oh, Virginia, you need a little food in your body to keep your spirit up," was the assistance's reply.

Mom did say that she liked her new room. She has a great view of the rose gar-den and her bed is next to the window. Her room was designed for three beds and she shares it with only one other lady. The staff hung Mom's pictures and moved her stuff. She kept talking about the party that was going on and the peo-ple that I invited into her home. "I would prefer if you would let me know when you plan to invite the entire neighborhood over to my house. You know my home is big, but not that big." She was truly a bit miffed that I hadn't given her advanced notice. I left her tonight giving the CNA the evil eye, as she attempted to shovel peas past Mom's lips.

SEPTEMBER

September 1, 2000

Dear James,

I talked to Mom this afternoon. She sounded strong and angry. Maybe frus-trated is a better word. She said she is still sick to her stomach. She sounded like her old Care Center self. Bye for now.

Love, Judy

September 1, 2000

She had a smirk on her face and her eyes sparkled. "I've done it now. I have brought down the Episcopal Church. I don't know how, but when they tried to make me believe like them … that did it." "Wow, Mom! That is really something," was my reply and my heart was warmed with seeing a bit of her fighting spirit return.

She spent much of the afternoon visit talking about Judy's and Katharine's phone calls. She told me that Katharine had told her that, "Steve had done something wrong. Yes he had. I don't know what it was, but when Judy called she knew about it, too. It was on the news you know. The local TV covered it on all the stations." Again I supported Mom and had her tell me more. She was never able to figure out what Steve had done, but it was definitely newsworthy.

She doesn't want to eat and spat up several times while I was there. I have always wondered where I got my amplified gag response and now I know. Mom can dry heave as good as I ever could, and I always thought I was the only one. She continues to view mealtime as her personal war. She and the aid, the poor woman, are locking horns at every meal. The CNAs must have some success, though, because Mom hates her for making her eat. Mom's eyes can crunch in against her nose and down towards her mouth in such a way that a poker chip could sit on the end of her nose and you wouldn't see anything but cheeks and forehead. I sure wouldn't what her looking at me with that chip on her nose.

September 2, 2000

Mom immediately, upon our entering her room, started to tell us about the long drive they made her take today. She had to use the potty, but was not given that opportunity. She said that she peed her pants. She peed her pants so badly that she was sitting in pee up to her thighs. She said, "I was so angry that they wouldn't stop. Then they let me sit in all that pee for hours. It got cold after a while, and I was embarrassed."

Suzanne and I visited with Mom twice today and the sitting in pee story was told both times. It must have been a hell of an experience. I tried to imagine how much urine it would take to fill a four-door car up to the height of one's thighs.

"You have got to check things out with me before you buy all of those buildings," she said. Mom wasn't happy that I had purchased more buildings and was spending all my time improving them. "You need to take better care of yourself. These properties take so much of your energy and time." I haven't purchased any properties, but trying to talk Mom out of what she knows is nigh impossible.

Mom reported that she had gotten into it with the high school music teacher and said, "I didn't like her in high school and I don't like her now. She is just too damn bossy." If I understand this one correctly, Mom's high school music teacher was not one of her favorite people. This woman, God only knows how, has shown up in the care center, and is still teaching music, and bossing Mom around.

She was probably in her 40's when Mom was in high school and would now be a little over 100. "My.... music is sure good for longevity," I thought. Apparently the years have had little impact on this teacher's attitude.

September 2, 2000

I visited with Mom three times today. She is weak and calling staff members bitches. It wasn't fun to be around her today. They are giving her yet another med to help her nausea. I feel bad that she wasn't well enough to go out. It might have helped her mood.

There are lots of times when my major role seems to be improving Mom's mood. There's nothing I can do about the strokes. There's nothing I can do about the falls. There's nothing I can do about the deterioration in her brain, or the loss of her husband, her home, her autonomy, her dignity. All I can give is time and some laughter. My son commented on that in a recent email.

September 3, 2000

Dad,

You know, as sad as Grandma's situation is at times, you bring such a sense of humor to it all. Your writing just makes me smile. Poor Grandma, up to her thighs in pee. What a bladder that woman must have! Did Grandma get my card yet? If so, did she like it? I'm sending another one Monday. Love ya!

The Son

September 3, 2000

Today I am anxious about the women in my life, and Mom is at the top of the list. I didn't see her until 4:00 p.m. The visit was not rewarding. I watched her talking with a staff member when I entered the building. I could see that Mom was grinding away on her. When the CNA spotted me, she quickly announced, "Look who is here!" and made her escape. I had wanted to hang back and just watch her for a bit, but that wasn't to be. "Hi, Mom. How are you?" I said. Her reply was, "What would you expect? They are all ganging up on me." I rolled her out on the patio and sat beside her. She began a twenty-minute rant about how mean everyone was and how she only had to answer to her husband and children. "I don't owe them an explanation about anything. If they don't know, I'm not telling them." I found myself holding my head in my hands, and turning down the volume of her voice.

I watched her hands, which are down to bone and tendon covered with a transparent drape of skin, reach out and snap dead leaves off of flower box plants. Her fingers were quick and agile. Her arteries pushed up under her skin, wandering like purple worms across one bone and then another. She is old.

Mom is eighty-one and her living has been reduced to a tired body in a wheel-chair managed by a mind that is not in touch with reality. I had hoped that the angry, hateful part of her had given way to acceptance and acquiescent. My wishes have not been granted. I hate seeing anger on her face, bitterness in her eyes and resentments in her mind.

I have not been taking very good care of myself lately. Before my trip to Yakima, to sell my parents' home and dismantle their belongings, I was good about praying daily and doing nurturing activities. I need to get back on track. If I don't take care of myself, I won't be any good for the women I love, or myself.

Mom's sickness, the recent falls and stomach problems, have improved. The nurse gave her a suppository of Phenergan yesterday afternoon at 4:30 p.m. and she had a better dinner. For days she has been sitting with a CNA who tries to feed her. At last they gave up and sat her at a window looking out at the garden. If she wants to eat, she can. No one is going to force the issue. This afternoon when I rolled her into the dining room she growled at the CNA as if she was a mortal enemy. I have never seen such nastiness in my mother. She's like a sick cornered cat that has been abused with a stick. She has won her battle and now they will leave her alone.

Today's entries are so dark. I have a need to sprinkle some sparkle on my thoughts. I do remember Mom holding my hand and her patting it. I taped all her cards on her new wall. "See, Mom. They love you," I said. There were cards from Greg, Jamie, Jackie, Jordan, Judy, Katharine and Bryan and letters from Inga, Anita, and other friends and family, who sent their love and support. Tomorrow, I will start my day with prayers and a good breakfast. I will then go visit Mom.

Dear Dad,

Yes, make sure you are saying your prayers and making time for you. It's so easy to let those things slide. Grandma might be around for years … really. Start making guidelines for your relationship with her. Yes, maybe you'll have to leave her alone more than you wish, and maybe you will feel like a bad guy. You're not, you know you're not, and you must take care of you to take care of others. I love you … Don't burn the candle at both ends. Love,

The Son

September 4, 2000

Mom got three cards today. She slowly read them to me. I was impressed with her vision and ability to read. Jordan's card was the easiest because it was computer generated and had large print. She also received cards from Ben and Audrey, her neighbors in Yakima, and her sister Katharine. She liked them all. "Oh, isn't it nice to get all these cards? Let's put them on the wall so I can look at them," she said. After posting the cards, we sat and talked while I sat in the slider chair, that was Mom's companion on her falls to the floor; and she in her wheel chair. I became aware, as we talked, that Mom was rolling her chair back and forth. With each roll she knocked her folded knees against my leg. She did it over and over, harder and harder. "Mom, are you mad at me?" I said. She dropped her forehead and gave me her evil eye. "Mom, that's the evil eye!" I shouted. "You damn rights it's the evil eye. I am mad at you. You keep making me go to all these things. I tell you to stop and you don't. How can I make you take me home? You put me in this place and you are keeping me here." "Oh, Mama!" I laughed. "I'm not keeping you here, and I'm not telling them to do anything." We talked on and on, but her attitude was locked in place. Today, I was the bad guy.

Towards the end of our visit she had to go to the bathroom. I rolled her up to the toilet and locked the wheels on her chair. I helped her slowly stand. Her legs shook, then she got her balance. I turned her and she pulled down her pants and slowly, almost missing the toilet, she sat. I stood there and she peed. At the end of it all she passed gas, looked up at me, raised her index finger and jammed it in my direction. She followed it up with another display of the evil eye. "Mom!" I said. She, with the indignation of a Queen, raised her head and wiped her bottom. Being with Mom in the bathroom is something that would have never happened in the normal years; and I had always thought that only the men in our family had gas. Tomorrow morning we are going to see her physician.

Judy continues to check up on Mom with phone calls and conversations to the staff. She is the manager of Mom's affairs, handling the finances, overseeing the services and assistance being provided, and doing all she can to participate in Mom's care. She, too, is concerned with how much Mom's illness is impacting my life.

Hi James,

I read your e-mail from last night and wondered if both Suzanne and Jamie are OK. Sure hope so. You better take good care of yourself, too. Mag still isn't over whatever he caught in Yakima. He still feels crummy some of the time. It seems to come and go.

I have gotten a couple of nurses on the phone the last few days. I think one of them was the one who you spoke of that comes on quite strong as to her evaluation of Mom's condition. I only talked to Mom briefly yesterday. She said that she was getting very dizzy and needed to hang up. So I did. In about five minutes, I called back to make sure she was OK. The nurse said she was sitting in her wheelchair drinking a milkshake and was fine.

Love Judy

Jordan joined in the advice and concerns with his emails.

Hi Dad,

Sounds wonderful … the prayers that is. I'm sorry this is all so heavy for you. Not sorry for you; just sorry that life does this to us. Supposed to make us stronger … I like the smaller short tests myself. This stuff is too rich in sadness to just shake off. It lives with you. Ahhhhhhhh, take a breath. Realize that this is the cycle of all things. Pat your dog. Think about your blessings, and taste the richness of all you have. Much Love,

The Son

September 5, 2000

I hate it. I hate it. I hate it. I have just returned from taking Mom to see her physician. She appears to be in pretty good health. He is upping her anti-depressant and cutting off the muscle relaxants. I will be attending a meeting for the family of Alzheimer's patients this afternoon at two. This morning my time with Mom was terrible. She's so damned angry. She's directing that anger towards me, with a toxic mix of, "I love you, and I know that you are doing the best you can, and I hate the life you are forcing me to live." She keeps talking about having a place of her own. She wants control of her life. She hates all those people who are trying to help her. She is sweet and tearful when she talks of being a burden for me; then refuses to enter the care center after the doctor's visit. She hangs on the door and won't let go. "Mom, we can't do this. I have to go to work. I can't leave you in the parking lot." "I won't go into that place. You can't force me to go where I don't want to go," was her cry. I pulled her hand from the door and rolled her chair into the lobby. I said, "Goodbye," and walked through the door. She was right behind me trying to force her way through the opening. I pushed her back and closed the door. I hate it. I hate it. I hate it.

I talked to staff when I returned for the support meeting. She said that Mom cried and cried when I left saying, "He will never come back."

The Alzheimer's support group session couldn't have come at a better time. I liked the meeting. There was a social worker, a member of the Care Center staff, a husband and a wife of Alzheimer's partners. I sat and listened to this husband and wife talk about behaviors that were identical to Mom's. They talked of their frustrations and fears. I left that group with a greater knowledge that Mom is not in control of herself. I must not engage in talk that leads to frustration. I need to change subjects or leave. The most loving thing I can do when I am not able to control my frustration with Mom is to say, "Mom, I gotta go. I will see you later." It isn't fair to fill Mom up with my frustrations. She has enough of her own. After the meeting I visited for a while with Mom. I told her that I was sorry, and she said the same. We hugged and held each other a little longer than normal. Our tears were shed on each other's shoulder.

September 7, 2000

I feel like I have just been washed up on the bank of a river following an accidental ride through unexpected white water. I am OK. I'm just too tired to pull myself up on the beach. I am pretty sure I could have avoided this adventure, if I had known what you do when you go for a ride on a white water river. In my support group I got information that will help me be more skillful in the future. I believe the problem started when I went to Yakima and returned with some of Mom's stuff. She didn't like it. Suzanne said that after our trip she and Mom talked when I was out of the room and Mom said, "You would think that they would wait until I was dead." I didn't hear about that conversation until the other night. What I did hear at the time was Mom being angry that I had taken control of her life and her possessions, and that I wasn't doing a very good job of keeping her happy. She was going to regain control and bring pressure to bear on me.

Today we had a sweet visit. She started to talk about getting out of the care center and I went with it. I am getting smarter. I have adopted the behavior of placing blame for things that are wrong in my Mother's life on anyone but me. Now the reason she is not able to leave is the doctor. He won't let her go. I would. He's the bad guy, not me. We talked about the home she would like and what steps we need to take to change the doctor's mind. I tell her that I will be delighted fix the place up, and she tells me all the things she would like.

She cries and talks about how hard it is living in the care center. I respond with, "Mom, what was the first car you and Dad owned?" Bam! Away went the tears and we were talking about a green Ford coupe. When I left today I felt better. I want to walk hand and hand with Mom down this path. If I have to be a liar on the way to keep her happier, lie I will. The truth brings her nothing but pain.

September 8, 2000

I painted Mom's nails today. They were uneven with a small patch of two week old polish in the center of each nail. After clipping them down and rounding them up, I applied a bright coat of pink polish. I didn't realize that the old purple patches from the last coat would show through and when they did I told Mom, "Wow! Your nails look like the fancy ones all the kids are wearing." She was pleased with the attention and didn't care how they looked. Our visit today was sweet. My new subject changing skills continue to be helpful. It is so easy to switch her to a subject that puts smiles on her face, rather than tears in her eyes.

September 9, 2000

I polished Mom's shoes this morning. She likes one pair of black loafers and as the days and weeks have passed, they have become splattered with food that hasn't made it to her mouth. It seems to be more important to me, than it is to her, that she looks clean and well groomed. Maybe she doesn't see how she looks. She does take pride in dressing herself in the morning, which is better than most of her hall mates.

When I picked her up this afternoon, after Suzanne and I had spent hours on the river fishing with no fish caught, Mom was extra happy to be out. We went directly to our house for lunch. Mom and Suzanne spent several hours gardening in the front yard, while I fell asleep. When I awoke the house was empty. Suzanne had taken Mom for a ride and then back to the care center. Mom wanted to go home to her bed and cried when Suzanne drove up to the care center's door. Home and the care center are two different places.

September 10, 2000

Thinking about Mom apart from attending to her physical and emotional needs is a luxury I am taking. I don't understand why but there is a difference in her eyes. They are darker and brighter. Her face is thin and the skin on her body is old. It feels good to hold her hand, to stroke her face, to kiss her cheek. There are times that she is like a young girl. I'm surprised that I see her this way with all the old that covers her exterior, but I do. There are smiles, turns of her head and ways that she uses her old hands that are so young, almost coquettish. She sees me as James, and sometimes John. Maybe I am being treated to a vision reserved for my father when he was young and they were together. It doesn't matter. I find delight in the moments. I know that a strong and capable woman has lived inside Mom's body. I see glimpses of her when she talks of moving to her little house. "It doesn't need to be much. I don't want a dump, but I don't need a lot. I want it to be clean with windows, lots of windows. It must have a garden filled with flowers, … the old fashioned kind that are mixed up. Do you know what I mean, James?" she said. "Yes," I say, "I know just the garden you are talking about." She goes on with, "and I will get one of the young girls in the family to come and live with me. They won't have to do anything, just be around to keep me company. I hate being alone. You know how I hate being alone." Mom's smile fades a little as she feels the wave of lonesomeness pass over her. She then, in an effort to change her mood, asked me for the third time, "What have you done so far today?"

September 10, 2000

It's raining today. Mom was in bed and was pleased to see me. We talked about my falling asleep yesterday. She said, "Your little woman was so nice. She drove me around for hours. You were pretty lucky with that one." We talked about her moving some day to her own little place. She was pleased to hear that most of her stuff was being stored by family and that, when she needed it, she could get it all back. She went on to say that she wanted to move back to Yakima, and that it was my turn to move with her. Our visit was longer than normal and during that time she would, as smooth as silk, move from me being her son to her husband and back. "You think so?" is my best reply, be I son or husband. When the time came for me to leave she said, "Take me with you." "Oh Mom, I have some things I need to get done and you wouldn't be safe." Her reply, "You sure are quick with the NO's when you don't want me around." I gave her a kiss, and was on my way.

September 11, 2000

Mom was in bed today. She talked about her confusion, "I do know that I often talk about things that are make-believe. Some times when I'm talking I find myself thinking, did this happen?" Mom was in a rattle-on-mode today. I said little while she talked and talked. When the staff came to take her to dinner she said, "I don't want to eat."

September 12, 2000

"Jamie, if you can come over here, you can sleep with me and we can eat Tootsie Roll Pops and watch TV." It was delightful to rock back in my chair and listen to Mom visit with my daughter on the telephone. She went on and on about Jamie's wedding and how happy she was for her. She promised to work on her health, so she could get out and attend the ceremony. Mom had lots of smiles and attracted the attention of her fellow patients with her laughter.

The social worker talked with me about Mom's not wanting to eat. At the care center, there are two rooms where patients eat. One is a regular dining room and all those who eat there feed themselves. The other is for those who are unable to feed themselves. They are spoon fed by the CNA's, with much mess and spillage. When Mom had her fall that made her nauseous and refused food for several days, she had been moved from the dining room to this other room. Now that she was more cognizant of others, she couldn't stomach the mess. I told the social worker that they still have Mom eating with the dependents, and that would quench any appetite. "Oh, I didn't realize that," was her reply. Soon she returned and said that tonight Mom would eat with her old friend Ruby, back in the regular dining room.

Ruby was sitting in her regular chair and glad to see Mom. There were two other new ladies there. When I introduced myself to them, they both extended their hands and said, "It's nice to meet you, James. You sure have a nice mother." They both talked and functioned on a level similar to Mom's. As I walked out of the dining room, all four were involved in full chitchat. It was nice to see. Maybe Mom will be a little more content with new friends.

September 13, 2000

"Lets go for a walk Mom!" She was sitting on her bed and was glad to hop into the wheelchair that I had rolled in front of her. "Oh, I am so glad to see you, James. Do I need a coat?" "No, Mom," I said, "its very warm outside today. The weather is perfect for a neighborhood walk." As we strolled Mom giggled at being outside. "Do you want to go into the department store?" was my question. "No, I want to be outside. I love being in the sunshine." We walked for forty-five minutes and during that walk we admired many a house and discussed Mom's current life problems. She has decided that she wants to move to Yakima and live with her sister. "I would be happy there, and it wouldn't be a problem at all for Katharine. She doesn't have anything else to do now that her children are grown." I replied with, "I wouldn't be too sure about that, Mom." When we returned to the care center, we sat on the front lawn and talked some more. She again presented her plan to move in with her sister, and I expressed my concern by saying, "Mom, you get angry when people who are trying to help you tell you what you need to do." "No, No," she said, "I don't do that anymore. I am sure that I would have no problem now that I appreciate how important it is to be free." "OK, Mom," I said, "We will see what we can do." I then rolled her into the care center.

I talked with Mom's physical therapist, who informed me that Mom is very capable of walking, but doesn't because she has a fear of falling. She wants Mom back in her walker. I talked with the treatment manager and asked her if she could set Mom up with a sponsor or sponsors who could take an hour or so a day to visit and walk with her. A family member of another Alzheimer's patient told me about the local volunteer program and it sounded great.

Mom was pretty happy as I rolled her into the independent dining room. When I said that I had to leave to cook dinner for Suzanne and myself she said, "Take me with you." I said, "I can't tonight, Mom." This made her mad. She tried to roll her chair away from the table. I had the tires locked and she was going to push herself over backwards if I didn't release them. "Mom, its time for your dinner," I said. She snapped back with, "I am not going to eat. I am going with you." I told her that we couldn't do it tonight. She turned, barking at me, "You are trying to boss me around more than your Dad." "My," I said, "What happened to that girl who wasn't going to get angry anymore?" Her friend Ruby looked at me and said, "Bye-bye," as she waved her hand. I took her counsel and left.

I had told my sister about the support group meeting I attended and how it gave me some new strategies for dealing with Mom. She decided to pursue the same and looked around in the Sacramento area for a group to attend.

Hi James,

I found a support group in our area that meets once a month. They won't be meeting for another few weeks. It sounds like Mom is getting stronger. Yesterday, a friend and I went into San Francisco for the day. We took the Amtrak from

Sacramento. In the city we got around on foot and by riding cable cars. We had a good time. Bye for now.

Love, Judy

September 14, 2000

When you walk down the hall at the Siuslaw Care Center, every few feet, there is a ten-foot section in the middle of the hall that is recessed. In that recessed section there are two doors on each side going into separate rooms. There is a space between those two doors where a chair sits. There is a chair on both sides of the hall. The chairs are alike and are padded with wooden arms. In the chair on the left side sits Ruby. She is always there. In the chair on the right side sits a new contender, my mother. Ruby is five feet tall and very round. She has tiny little feet that appear to be little more than toes on the extension of her ankle. Every thing about Ruby is round including her head, which has large full lips and pregnant eyes. Her hair is red, curly and parted on the top. Ruby only moves when it's time for eating. She walks with the help of a walker. Mom likes Ruby. She likes her a lot. There is an expressed pact between them and they support each other. They watch what happens and they talk. When I sit and visit with Mom in the hall, Ruby listens. When Mom is funny, Ruby laughs. When Mom is angry, Ruby's eyes give me permission to leave.

September 15, 2000

Sitting in the sunshine on the care center patio, Mom prattled on and on about how she disliked the place, the staff and the loneliness. I made a decision, some time back, that I wouldn't try to change her. I would always support her in all her thoughts and fantasies. Some times I am successful; others, I am not.

"I can't wait to get out of this place. There is no one here that I can talk with. Come on, James, get me out of here," she pleaded over and over. "Gosh Mom, you seem to really enjoy your time with Ruby," I said. "She is OK," Mom said, "but she's getting ready to die. I can tell by looking at her." "But, Mom," I said, "what about your new lady friends that you have dinner with every night? Why don't you try to build a better relationship with them?" "They are not my kind of people," she said, "They don't have anything in common with me. I just want to get out of this place and have a little spot of my own." "Who would care for you Mom? Who would be willing to stay with you in your own place, and what would keep you from getting angry with them like you have with all the others that have cared for you?" I said. She snapped around with, "Now don't you get bossy with me. I can get along with anyone."

I'm hooked by Mom's unhappiness and believe I have been mistaken in leading her to believe that she would be leaving the care center someday. She needs to appreciate that this is the best place for her. "Mom," I said, "the doctor believes that this is the very best place for you. He believes that you aren't and won't be able to safely live outside of a place like the care center. You have Alzheimer's, and it will slowly keep taking little parts of your memory away. You need to figure out things that you can do here that will bring you happiness. You need to make friends here. You need to let go of the thought that you are going to get a whole bunch better and move into a place of your own. You … I am sorry, Mom. I so want you to be happy, and you so often aren't." "Have you said enough, Mr. High and Mighty?" she said, "I won't stay here!!" "OK, Mom," I said, and walked her back to her room, where she sat on the bed. Ruby was sitting in the hall. I pulled another chair out so they could sit by each other. "Mom's mad at me, Ruby. Will you watch out for her for a while?" "Sure" she said with a big smile.

I know that logic will not make Mom happy. Nothing can make her happy. The day I can accept that, I will probably be a better supporter of her and more at peace with myself.

I told Judy that Mom received her book Thursday and the entire staff loves it. Judy had sent Mom a coffee-table book with beautiful pictures. It gave her something to show off or to start conversations. Several of the staff spent time looking at it with her. Mom was pleased that Judy sent it.

September 17, 2000

There is a game they play in the halls of the Siuslaw Care Center that I have never seen before. Today, when I visited Mom, I had to pause as I walked down the hall to her room. Two women, who had left their voices and the control of much of their bodies in the early days of their disease, were facing each other. They were in wheelchairs and appeared to be angry. The woman closest to me had her leg resting on a brace that was attached to her chair and left it protruding like a knight's lance. Her head always road on her shoulder and she kept her small doll tucked close to her chest. I knew her to be a real sweetheart who loved Elvis.

The other woman had her hair cropped short and, although wordless, her anger around her disabled condition could be noticed at a casual glance. She had just smashed her chair into the side of the Elvis lady and rolled down the hall where she turned around. I had watched her smash many a patient and I had, on several occasions, been a victim of her attacks.

The ladies were looking directly into the others eyes and there was no movement. I froze with my back against the wall as the woman with the lance like leg placed her one good hand on the wheel of her chair. She began rolling and even though the angry lady attempted to roll her chair to the side of the hall she wasn't able to avoid her opponent's elevated and braced foot, which smashed the side of her chair and spun her to the side and out of the way. In victory, the Elvis lady continued to roll down the hall without the slightest glance behind.

September 18, 2000

I wondered if Mom had noticed that I didn't visit yesterday. She was parked in the middle of the hall as I turned the corner. She had no facial expression. "Good morning, James. How are you?" Ohhhhh, so cool was her look and voice. "Good, Mom, how about you?" I asked. "Pretty good, considering I haven't had a visitor in over three days," she said. "Are you mad that I didn't visit yesterday?" I asked. "Only yesterday?" she said. "It seemed like at least three days." She spent a few minutes letting me know that she had noticed that I hadn't visited, then we went on to our normal set of questions. She patted me on my knee, and talked about how glad she was that she had Ruby as a friend.

Mom and I went for an afternoon drive. She always loves getting out. Today it was smooth, with no stressful moments. Sometimes I think that she forgets everything of the day before; at other times, I know she knows. On our last few visits she talked about moving to another place, but today the moving talk has dwindled to nothing. She even asked what hobby she could develop that would make the passing of time more enjoyable. Her negative talk about the care center and the staff did not come up. She also made statements like, "If I can find just one friend, I will be OK."

I discovered another support group named Elder Help. I have heard that they have people who want to visit with and help folks like Mom. Wouldn't it be great if some old gal tied up with Mom and would take her out for little daily excursions?

September 19, 2000

Today's visit was a bit of a mixed bag. Mom was happy to see me, and to spend some time on the patio in the sunshine. She also moved into a few moments of tears with, "I can't believe that I had three children, and not one of them had an old wood shed out back for me to stay in." "SHIT," I said. The ultimate bad kid statement. When she thought I looked like I had been shot in the gut, she said, "Oh, don't get yourself upset. Can't an old woman complain without you getting upset?"

I had an opportunity to speak with the director of Elder Help. Her name was Mandy, and she said that she had several ladies that would love to spend time with Mom. She would set it up. Good.

September 20, 2000

We had two visits today and both were pleasurable. Mom was in good spirits most of the time. When I left her after our morning visit she said, "Aren't you taking me home?" I said I had to work, but would be back in the afternoon. She became tearful and frustrated. She spun her chair around and rolled away crying.

This afternoon we went for a drive, and enjoyed it a lot. We can tour through the same neighborhoods over and over, and she is always excited. She has not yet had a visitor from Elder Help. I do hope that works out. Yesterday I told Mom that they had placed the stone on Dad's grave. She said, "That's good. It feels done, doesn't it? I hope the family likes it." I gave Mom a kiss, and was out the door feeling good.

September 21, 2000

Hi James,

I had a good visit with Mom on the phone last night. You were right. She was having a good day. I almost called you after I visited with her. She remembered her comment about her three kids and a little shack! She brought it up and asked me if you had said anything about it. She knew that it had upset you. Also, she told me about your ride yesterday. Her memory surprised me last night. She was doing quite well. She doesn't understand why family and friends don't come and visit her. She talks a lot about you and the sixty-mile drive you have to make every time you visit her. She has you far away like the rest of her family and friends. She joked and laughed some. I hope she has more of those days. Would you let me know if you received this note? It is the first time I have used your new email address. Also, do you have any suggestions for a wedding gift for Jamie?

Love, Judy

September 21, 2000

I visited with Mom in the late afternoon. Her spirits were good and she cried over the death of Dad. She said, "I find, now that I am spending more time in bed, that I think of your father a lot. It makes me sad and I don't want to cry." She also said, "I feel myself slipping." "What does that mean, Mom?" I asked and she said, "Oh, I don't know exactly what it is. I just know that I am slipping a little each day." We ended our visit with a smile and a kiss.

September 22, 2000

Hello James,

I have a question. I bought a little bookcase yesterday for Mom. It has four shelves. I noticed when we were at the care center that she had very little space to set anything on. I thought it could be an early Christmas gift. We could bring it to Mom when we visit in October. Do you think this would be OK? It isn't very deep. Let me know what you think. I can take it back if you think it is a bad idea.

Love, Judy

Sweet Sister,

The bookcase sounds good. She could put lots of little things on it that would remind her of better times.

Little brother

Today Mom and I sat on the back patio and talked. It was mid-morning, and I had less than an hour to visit. She has taken to smiling when I arrive. She gives me a quick peck, and then we talk. She told me that I must have had quite a party last night, and that Ruby was tired this morning from all her playing around. She thought that my getting Ruby back at 4:00 a.m. was a bit too late. I told her that I didn't have a party, nor did I have Ruby out. "You see, that's what is wrong with me. I can't trust my own mind anymore," she said.

September 24, 2000

I picked Mom up mid-morning and brought her to our house. I pulled out the piano stool and she played for along time. I made a video of her as she enjoyed herself. Early in the afternoon we attended the Florence Chowder Blues and Brews. It's a local festival with great blues and lots of tasty sea food. The beer drinkers are treated to new brews the area brewers have created.

Mom was in her wheelchair and we rolled her to a good spot where she ate shrimp sandwiches and enjoyed the music. The bands played lots of old songs from the big-band era which Mom loved. It took her back to happier, spry times when she frolicked with friends. On the way back to the care center Mom said, "Why don't I go home with the two of you? I will only stay until tomorrow, then you can take me back to the care center." I didn't take her up on her idea. I knew that someday I will say, "Why didn't I take her home for just that one night?"

September 25, 2000

Mom was happy to see me this morning. We enjoyed a short visit while she talked about how loud my nightly parties were, and wondered if I would be having them every night. "It wouldn't be so bad if you would invite me," she said. Judy called and Mom quickly rolled down the hall to talk with her. She's always delighted when the CNA says, "Virginia, you have a call."

September 26, 2000

It's a ZOO. I hear Mom's voice as I walk down the hall, "No, honey. This isn't your room. I don't know where your room is. Now, now don't cry. We will find your room." "Her room is outside by the trees," yells Ruby who is watching Mom play Florence Nightingale. "That is right," says Mom, "your room must be outside. I have seen you go that way often." Ida, the ninety-two year-old woman again drops her head and cries, "This is my room. This is where I sleep." I sit down in the empty hall chair, and Mom keeps talking to Ida. Ida, through her tears, says to Mom, "I can't hear. Talk louder." Mom leans closer and Ruby yells,

"She can't hear." Mom puts here mouth against Ida's ear and says, "This isn't your room." Ida again drops her head and cries. "What's the problem, Mom," I ask. "This poor old girl," Mom says, "thinks that this is her room, and I keep pushing her back out into the hall. She is not going to find her way if she keeps coming into my room. She has been doing this for hours and I can't get her to move on." "Mom," I said, "she is your roommate."

September 27, 2000

Mom has returned to, "I'm sorry, but you are my husband and you aren't giving me enough attention. I dislike your not following my rules and messing around with other women." I had hoped that these days had passed, but they haven't. Any man who has blown it with his wife would have recognized the expression on Mom's face.

September 28, 2000

Today Mom was queen of the phones. When I arrived she was finishing up her conversation with Judy and five minutes later was on the phone again, this time with her sister, Katharine. I love seeing her get the calls. People who are not right in the midst of a person's struggle with Alzheimer's cannot imagine how helpful it is to have reminders that they are not forgotten. I have so much gratitude in my heart for all the friends and family members who called or sent cards and letters. Not only did it do a great deal to lift Mom's spirits, but it made me feel supported, too. Thank you!

September 29, 2000

Hi James,

The video of Mom playing the piano didn't arrive today. I'm looking forward to seeing it. Mom has been talking about how she confuses you with Dad, and what a fool she feels like. She says she doesn't know what's true and what is not. I do feel so sorry for her. Do you think she could use a nice hair cut in case she is able to go to the wedding? I don't have any special plans for the weekend. Hope all is well at your house.

Love, Judy

September 30, 2000

Suzanne and I attended Jamie's bridal shower in Eugene, and then, when we got back to Florence, visited with Mom. She was upset and as hard as she tried to stay on top of her despair and tears, she couldn't. Our visit was filled with her self-pity and powerlessness. I shared and appreciated her feelings.

Immediately following our visit, Suzanne drove me to the hospital. I was having numbness in my left arm and the left side of my tongue. I also had some mild chest pains. They gave me the full treatment x-rays, EKG, blood tests and the rest of the la-te-da's that are part of a heart check up, and I tested OK. I had triple by-pass surgery at age forty-four, so I am on medications for heart disease and keep a careful watch out for signs that my heart might be malfunctioning. This time the verdict is anxiety, not heart problems. Good. It seems I accept far too much responsibility for the happiness of others, and hold myself very accountable.

I found out Friday that someone from Elder Help will be visiting with Mom. I don't know how often they can visit, but hope that it's at least several times a week. I'm making it my goal to manage my feelings more effectively this next month. Killing myself in an attempt to support my mother isn't my life goal. I hate this.

OCTOBER

October 1, 2000

I spent most of Sunday attending a meeting in Roseburg, 90 miles from home, and didn't see Mom. I'm always anxious when I miss a day. I can plan on her being mad, and I don't like that.

October 2, 2000

"I know I am hard on you son. You look tired. Are you OK?" I sat with Mom while she cried. I must have looked melted and she noticed. From somewhere inside her, she again, as she has for my entire life, set aside her problems to focus on mine. I talked about how hard it is for me to see her unhappy and how powerless I am to make her life better. Today she rose above her own tears and said, "It's OK, Son, don't you worry."

October 3, 2000

Judy has talked with Mom (I can tell) and now Mom is trying to protect me. Judy must have told her about my anxiety attack and the trip to the hospital. Mom is guarded, not wanting to say or do anything that will cause me discomfort. My inability to deal with Mom's disease is now impacting all of us. I must transcend the disease and be a joyful and happy being. It serves no good for me to flounder under this test.

October 4, 2000

"The nurse told me about my condition and it's not good news," Mom said. It was a serious start to our visit. I could tell by her expression she was upset. "What did the nurse tell you Mom?" I asked. "She said that I will be here for the rest of my life, and there was no hope that my condition would improve." "Oh, Mom," I said, "What do you feel about what she said?" "I didn't like it one bit." she said, "Although she may be right. I know that I am weaker, my vision is failing and I'm become more confused every day. I just wish I could spend my time in a place that felt like home." We changed the topic and talked for a while about happier things. When it came time for me to leave, she was better.

I attended my monthly support group and afterwards visited with Mom for a few minutes. She was seeing me as Dad, and was angry that I wasn't taking better care of her. I kissed her and told her that I would come by tomorrow.

October 5, 2000

I listened to PBS radio station this morning. They were talking about Alzheimer's and techniques that have proven to be effective. Avoiding conflict and being agreeable was the recommended practice. So when Mom tells me about all the people who have been visiting her during the night, I should just smile and say, "Wow! Was it a nice visit?" Sometimes it makes me feel schizophrenic to deal with reality in the rest of my life, and to submit to the fantasy of Mom's mind when I am with her.

October 6, 2000

Mom was not a very nice lady today. She was not very nice at all. I had to make a drive up to Reedsport this morning to do some minor repairs on a house, and thought that it would be fun to get Mom out and have some visit time. I was trying to kill two birds with one stone. Mom was ashen in color and her expression was that of a young girl who had just discovered that her dog didn't run away, you had shot it. "Hi, Mom, do you want to go for a little working drive with me? "I will do anything it takes to get out of this place," she said, "even riding with you." Most people would have interpreted Mom's attitude at this point as poor. Putting yourself in the confines of a truck cab would be a mistake. I didn't, so I did experience two hours of "Why did you leave me? How long have you been married? Why did you sneak behind my back? How do you think this makes me feel?" And my favorite, "Do you still love me?" It was an extra beautiful day with blue skies, clouds and sunshine. I don't believe Mom noticed much of it. I was proud when I returned her to the care center and walked away without the regular knot in my gut.

October 7, 2000

It was a sad visit again today. Mom was in a desperate mode and didn't move from that position. She was stuck on my being Dad. "Why did you marry her? I didn't know about it. How do you like living with all her kids? It would be better if I could hate you, but I love you." The visit could have been longer, but I cut it short and escaped while I was still in one piece. I don't think I will visit for a day or two.

October 13, 2000

I have been away from writing for several days. Judy and Mag arrived in town Wednesday and they have spent lots of time with Mom. New clothes and things to make Mom's room more beautiful are appearing. It's nice to have my sister here. I like it when she shares her observations. Today we will drive to Eugene and tomorrow my daughter, Jamie, will marry.

Judy is thinking about taking Mom to the wedding. Both Judy and I know that Mom would like to attend, but have concerns around her stamina. She continues to slide deeper into her world of fantasy and would win first prize in any story telling contest. She can talk non-stop about her daily experiences, even though she hasn't left her room. She tells of her downtown adventures with half of the patients being involved with the police, city hall, and then being arrested. She seems very pleased with her personal accounts.

October 18, 2000

So much has happened. Yesterday when I visited Mom she was angry that we hadn't shown up to take her out to dinner and home. She was unable to get over her anger so I kissed her and left. She continues to complain about all of us going off to play, and her being stuck with all the kids. We did take Mom to Jamie's wedding. She liked getting dressed up. She rode with Judy & Mag, so they could leave if she got tired, but she held up well. She was great at the wedding. She loved all the excitement and was pretty easy to care for. Several of my friends reported talking with her and being impressed at her good health.

Judy and Mag had to go back home. They left the day after the wedding and Mom is suffering the adjustment back to normalcy. While Judy and Mag were here, Mom got lots of outings, had lots of company, and loved every moment. I feel bad that I am unable to keep up that social pace for her.

I visited with the woman from Elder Health and she seems very interested in taking Mom out for coffee and giving her the chance to complain about her circumstances. What a kind act.

October 19, 2000

Dear Judy,

I asked Mom today if she was interested in being involved with the Shorewood Alzheimer group and she said, "Yes." She also talked about her new lady friend, the volunteer from Elder Help, and how much she enjoyed her. My visit this morning with Mom was good. She was in the process of putting some of her clothes away. She told me that she didn't watch her TV, so I could take it away, if I wanted to.

I paid the beautician to cut and set Mom's hair. She had given Mom a great cut. It had only been six weeks or so since Mom had a perm, and her hair had lots of body. Listen to me talk "girl talk."

She was extremely confused today with parties, children, noise and her going here and there. She complains that there are so many children around the care center, and that she is in charge of their care. Sometimes she doesn't mind, but it is so much work. It really tires her out. She shouldn't have to do it all! These children belong to the staff one day, then the next, she is their school teacher, then yet another day, she teaches Sunday School to them. I try to remain neutral, not contradicting her stories, but there is a glimpse of understanding in her eyes as she says, "Sometimes, I don't trust my own thinking."

James

October 20, 2000

She was slumped to the side as she sat in her hall chair that she and Ruby used like two lions guarding holy ground. She tells me that she spends most of her day sitting in the hall. There's a lot of action in the hall and Mom keeps a watch on much of it. She is still upset with Ruby. She had decided that Ruby wants to move into her room and probably eat her food, Ruby being so fat and such. "I just can't let it happen. I feel bad that she doesn't have people, but she isn't my responsibility. When you get to my age, you learn that you have to take care of yourself." She turned her head towards me and gave me one of those you-have-let-me-down looks and said, "No one else will!!!"

Today, as I sat beside her, I heard this kind of talk. "Why in the world do they do that? Those people downstairs should know that I can't be responsible for all those children. Some of them are still in diapers and I don't want to be changing them. The girls keep running around with their heads cut off, and I know why. They didn't keep the payments up, and they are going to lose their car. I have worried and worried about that and now there are stains everywhere. Where were you last night? I could hear you whooping it up. I would think that you would get tired of those women. How many kids do they have living in my house?" After all her complaints, she looked me in the eye and wiped the tapioca pudding off her fingers onto my pants.

October 24, 2000

I didn't see Mom today. I guess that's OK. I had to attend classes this morning to deal with my diabetes and this afternoon was filled with cleaning the house for a Baha'i Fireside. Mom has been mellow lately. She seems more content in her environment. The world her mind lives in is very active, even if her body doesn't get to go along. I think that's a blessing. I do understand that a day will come when she will fully step into that world, and leave us all behind to attend to her body. I continue to have such mixed feelings around her illness and the demands she places on us. It would be wonderful to give her true peace and contentment. I wish I could. I know I can't.

October 26, 2000

I had a nice visit with Mom this morning. She said that she is enjoying her TV very much. "I like to turn the volume up in the afternoons, so the other people will know what I am watching." She is sitting in her glider chair and watching TV when I walk in. "Hi, James, how are you? Are you working hard today?" We talked about a lot of things. I told her that Judy and I would like her to spend Thanksgiving in Sacramento with Judy and her family. I would drive her there on my way down to LA to see Jordan and pick her up on the way back. She said, "Oh good. Now I have something to look forward to." I also told her that her sister would be in Florence next Wednesday and would be able to spend a bunch of time with her. Mom was pleased that Katharine was coming and said, "What's she doing? One last visit before I die?"

I talked to the staff about Mom's bladder problems and asked them to check her out. Mom said she thinks things are coming out where they shouldn't.

October 27, 2000

Mom fell tonight. They say she is fine. They found her sitting on her bedroom floor. She said her hip hurt. They say she is fine. They called the doctor and told him that she was OK. I understand that she has been walking in socks. Today she held up a banana and asked me if I lost something. She then winked. MOM!

October 29, 2000

It was a strange visit with Mom today. She smiled and was happy to see me. We sat in her room and talked about Jamie's new house and how delighted she is with her new life. Mom was pleased with that information and talked about her feeling at this time of her life. "All of you kids are OK, and I am of no value. Why are you making all these efforts to keep me here? I have no reason to live and, if I am not going to recover from this illness, I would rather not live." "Does it scare you to think about dying Mom?" I asked. "It used to, but not any more," she said. "I don't understand why you say you are so worried about my well being. If

I can't have a normal life, let me go." We talked about and around this subject for most of the visit. Mom cried at times and was sweet with smiles at others. I left her watching King Kong, the 1940 version.

October 30, 2000

When I popped in to see Mom this morning they were taking her to the doctor to have her checked out for the fall and the problem the urologist dealt with two years ago. She was confused and was a bit tearful. I kissed her and promised to be back later. When I returned she was in good spirits. She said that they had to sit in the doctor's office for two hours. The aid that took her, who is the older lady that was Mom's teacher in high school and Mom dislikes, said that it was true. I think it is a bad deal when old people have to wait for appointments.

Mom seems to have mixed emotions about Katharine coming. She's happy one moment, and uninterested the next. I am anxious to watch the union. There are lots of interesting dynamics between two sisters. I made a mistake and let Mom walk me to the door, where she jammed her walker into the opening and attempted an escape. "They can't keep me prisoner here. I can leave if I want." An aid came to my rescue.

October 31, 2000

It's Halloween today and I am sitting at my desk in my office making notes as I listen to my mother play the piano. She plays and plays and seems OK being alone. I'm impressed with her ability. Judy bought her a book of big print sheet music, which seems much easier for her to play.

Katharine should be arriving soon and I thought that it would be nice for the sisters to meet away from the care center, so I brought Mom over to my place, and gave Aunt Katharine my address. The care center feels like what it is. It will be fun to watch Katharine and Mom together.

NOVEMBER

November 1, 2000

I saw my mother this morning. I asked her how her evening was. She responded with, "same as always." I asked her if she remembered going out to dinner with Katharine, Keith, Kristi, Tom, Suzanne and I. She said, "Oh, yes, I do remember that." She said that she loved seeing Katharine and that she so missed her life. So much has changed for Mom. She has left everything she knew behind herself and is living a life that is not of her choosing.

Mom was sitting at the piano when her sister walked in. She had been playing for a good hour with her eyes closed much of the time and her hands moving to the memories of the music. When Katharine walked to Mom's side, Mom covered her mouth with her hands and cried. She did not take her eyes off her sister.

We spent the afternoon talking and when we decided to go out for dinner Mom was tired. She came with us and was quiet as we enjoyed the Chinese cooking at The Lotus, which sits on the banks of the Siuslaw River. We drove Mom back to the care center and signed her in. Her aides were quick to welcome her and swish her off to her room, and her comfortable bed. Mom was very tired. Katharine and family plan to take Mom out for lunch today. I enjoyed the visit with family very much. Getting to know Kristi and Tom better was a pleasure and being around my sweet uncle and aunt was great. I directed them towards the beach for an early morning walk before picking Mom up. Mom said, "It will be nice to go to lunch with them. I wished she lived closer."

November 2, 2000

Today will be Mom's first day in her Alzheimer's group. She said that she had a good time having lunch with Katharine, and that she sure misses family. Her spirits were good and she talked about how pleased she was that she had that surgery to remove that golf ball sized growth, and now she could urinate more easily. She was also amazed that she has had no pain from the surgery. I wondered where this idea had come from. Later I picked Mom up and off we went to her Alzheimer group. It is only five blocks away from the care center, and Mom was feeling good. When we arrived we were directed to a room down the hall. Upon entering there were probably twenty people sitting around tables playing games, drinking coffee, tea and visiting. Within moments Mom was a part of the action. There were smiles all around and the women who offer the program were attending to the needs of the group. When I asked Mom if it would be OK for me to leave she offered a quick, "Sure, Honey."

November 3, 2000

Mom was sweet today. Our visit was without occurrence. We sat in her room with her on the bed and me in her slider. We talked about Katharine's visit and how the kids are doing. She did discuss several times all the parties I have been having and wondering why Ruby was always invited.

November 5, 2000

I rode my bike down to see Mom. Today's visit was much like what I had fantasized having Mom near-by would be like. She was happy to see me as she putted about her room. I sat in the slider and she on the bed, like we have become accustomed. Our visit began with, "How is everybody?" We then talked about her moving and what she wanted. I don't discourage her much and keep reminding her of how much she is loved at the care center. "All your little helper girls wouldn't be able to see you if you lived in a house away from here." We also talked about my brother's death. She said that her most powerful feelings around Steve's death were embarrassment and concern over what he had done to himself in the eyes of God. She went on to say that she didn't think he was in his right mind, but he sure wasn't going to let anyone help him. We then talked about Dad's father, Frank, who she described as "a grabber and everyone knew it." She said that when Dad was gone to war, he would come over and chase her around the place. She said that she had to become mean-as-hell to keep him in his place. "Why are men that way?" she asked. "I don't know Mom. I sure hope I'm not that way when I'm old." "Well if it turns out that you are, you come over to my place and I will cut it off for you." "OK," I said with a quick smile. She also talked about the Alzheimer's group and how it's OK but playing cards and putting puzzles together isn't her idea of a twice a week thing. "Maybe once a week would be enough," she said. Today's visit ended with a promise to see her later and her saying as she patted her hands together, "Good, oh, good. I will see you later then."

It was a very nice afternoon with Mom. Suzanne and I needed to run some school supplies up to Newport and Waldport, a hundred mile round-trip. We took Mom along in the pickup and had a grand time. It was clear and beautiful on the way up, and dark and rainy on our way back. We sang lots of old songs. Mom must have got us all going on "Home on the Range" a half dozen times. We had a nice meal of fish and chips in Waldport and delivered Mom back to the care center tired and happy.

November 7, 2000

Hi James,

I asked Mag about the time it would take to drive from Sacramento to L.A. He thought it would be a short seven hours. That is about an hour less than I thought it was. Give Jamie our best. I am very happy for her. I talked to Mom yesterday afternoon. It sounded like she was having a bad day. She was angry and unhappy. Her state of mind keeps changing! I better get ready to vote! Bye for now.

Love, Judy

Sweet Sister,

I am surprise that Mom was angry and unhappy. When I visited with her yesterday morning she was happy, or at least OK. She didn't want to go to her Alzheimer's group. She said that all they do is play card games and puzzles. I will take her back Thursday and let them know her feelings and see if they can just pop her in a group with gals who like to talk. That is all Mom really wants to do—talk.

James

Mom sits on her side of the hall and Ruby is on the other. They smile and begin the mean game. I do not know how long they have been playing this game or how often it is played. I do know that I was watching this morning, and was amazed at the aggressiveness of this nursing home sport. Ruby starts with, "I don't know why you have to lie about everything. You are so nice to his face and say all those things behind his back. I think it would be better if you just let him know what you think of him." Mom slides a little down in her chair, not to cower, but rather to brace herself for her turn. "I don't agree with you at all. Even if you are upset with someone, it is better to tell a little lie that to hurt their feelings." Ruby rolls her head to the side and talks like a judge placing sentence upon a criminal. "You liars are all the same. You lie to yourselves and everyone else." I know that I am the subject of this argument and that Mom is attempting to sidestep this attack. "Well Ruby, some of us want to be nice to others and you are mean hearted. I bet you have never had a friend who stuck around very long for your mean honesty." They tossed barbs back and forth for several minutes until a staff nurse interrupted and told them to be nice to each other. "Ruby, you are being mean to Virginia because she won the Best Patient of the Month Award and you are jealous." Ruby gave her a sneer and told Mom that she had half of the thing done and when it was finished she was going to give it to Mom and that would teach her a lesson. Half of what I had no idea. Mom handed me the last half of her sandwich and asked me to give it to Ruby. Ruby said, "for me?" and began to eat it. Mom said, "She has diabetes, and I hope it kills her." I gave Mom a kiss and left, knowing that her day was at least going to be interesting.

Sweet Sister,

I am very interested to find out more about Hodgkin's syndrome. I didn't attend this month's Alzheimer's support meeting. There are only three of us there and the other two are a husband and wife who are supporting their partners at home. They use up group time in understandable processing. I appreciate their need for that process, but would have liked more information and education Suzanne got the 22nd of November off so we can travel on Wednesday and deliver Mom to you by dinner time. Can we sleep over? We will hit the road very early Thursday morning to arrive at Jordan's in the early afternoon for Thanksgiving dinner.

James

November 8, 2000

Hi James,

I went to a support group meeting last night. I got two hours with one of the facilitators. She is very knowledgeable, and is doing research in Alzheimer's. I learned a lot. I will call you soon and fill you in. It sounds like Mom may have Hodgkin's syndrome, if I understand it correctly. The researcher said that it is Alzheimer's related. The backward arching she does, dryness of mouth and shuffling of the feet are classic signs of the problem. There is nothing to do about it. It just explains why it is happening. There is medication out there to stop the progression of Alzheimer's. Will talk to you soon.

Love, Judy

November 9, 2000

Today's visit with Mom was interesting. She's OK with Ruby again, and said, "Oh, she gets herself on her high horse sometimes, but she has a good heart. You know she doesn't have any family." We talked a bit more about our Thanksgiving trip and her moving to another place. Judy and I talked last night about all the information she gained at her Alzheimer's meeting. She is going to explore possible meds that may be helpful for Mom.

November 13, 2000

Mom was not in good spirits today. She tried to be nice and failed. Everyone and everything was not to her liking. Her hair was also a mess. I have noticed that when her bad days come she lets you know with her presentation. She didn't seem to notice that I hadn't been around for a couple of days. Maybe she did notice and that was the reason for the poor mood.

November 19, 2000

I showed up at the care center around lunch time, and found Mom in the dining room. She didn't have her glasses on. When I asked her about them, she said that she had left them on the counter at the new department store. She said, "I drove down there this morning and some time during my shopping I laid the glasses down and didn't pick them back up." The staff said that they had done a search and had not been successful yet. "They will show up in a day or two. They always do," I was told by the RN. Mom pointed out a poor old fellow across the room who was eating and not doing a great job of it. "Someday that will be you," she said, "it will be your chance to find out how much fun it is being old." Our visit was OK and we talked about our trip to Sacramento. She said that she would get a CNA to help her pack her bags.

The trip to Sacramento for Thanksgiving was good. Mom was a great traveler. She marveled at the scenery and we sang old songs. She dozed off a few times. When we got to Judy & Mag's house, she was happy to see them. She expressed a little concern that Suzanne and I were not staying on for the holiday, when I explained that we were driving on to Jordan's house, but I assured her that she would be with Judy and her family and they would take good care of her.

Our time in Los Angeles was a wonderful respite for me. I suffered no remorse for leaving Mom at my sister's house and had fun being fancy-free with my son and his friends.

When we arrived back at Judy's to pick Mom up and take her back to Florence, Mom told Judy how she didn't want to go, then told me never to leave her somewhere strange like that for such a long time. Poor confused Mama!

November 28, 2000

Hi James

The memory medication is ARICEPT. I am anxious to hear what the doctor has to say about Mom's tipping back! I visited with Gail today. Where her Mom is staying, they have a doctor's evaluation of the Alzheimer patients two or three times a year. It would be good to have an evaluation of Mom's condition. Bye for now.

Love, Judy

DECEMBER

December 1, 2000

Suzanne and I had Mom over for my birthday dinner. She spilled two cups of coffee and one glass of water. She seems very detached from her body. I talked with the staff about Mom's instability and leaning backwards. They said that if she is left to herself she does pretty well with her balance. If you attempt to help her she transfers her balance to the person who is helping her, and has a difficult time. I have watched her move about the past few days and she does do well until I offer her help. We had fun last night. Mom's spirits were high and her humor was good.

December 2, 2000

Hi James,

HAPPY BIRTHDAY!!!!! Sorry I didn't remember. I lost track of dates! Glad you had a good day, Old Man. I called Mom's doctor today. I left questions with the receptionist and the nurse called me back. The doctor is making rounds at the care center this weekend. He will check out Mom's backward tilt and the Aricept medication thought. It didn't sound like the medication would be a good idea at this time. Even if Mom only goes backward when someone is helping her, it still seems like a strange way to loose your balance. We should get feedback on the doctor's visit next week. Did Mom get a perm on Thursday? I called and the hairdresser said that she could give her a perm yesterday afternoon.

Judy

Hi Judy,

Good for you. I am anxious to hear what the doctor has to say. When I popped in on Mom this morning there were three aids visiting with her. She was sitting in her glider chair, one aid was on her bed, another in a near by rocking chair, and one on the other bed. They were just having a visit with their favorite patient. I love that. It looked like a high school sleep over.

Mom's hair is curly. Mom's hair is very curly. She said that it would loosen up in a few weeks. She's happy and looks much like a poodle dog.

James

December 6, 2000

Hi James,

I talked with the charge nurse at the care center this morning. The doctor did see Mom this weekend. Her chart said no change in medications. No comments as to our concerns about the leaning backwards. I was told you have to be assertive with the doctors. They are very busy so … I will give the doctor's office a call tomorrow. The nurse said vertigo, which is common with older people, can cause this balance problem. Bye for now.

Love, Judy

December 9, 2000

There have been many untold stories and observances this past month and little has been written about them. Mom is doing fine. She's much happier since she spent the holiday with Judy and Mag in Sacramento. Judy said that after spending a few days with her, Mom knows how good she had it at the care center. Mom did do very well on that trip. The drive up and back was nine plus hours and she did as well or better that Suzanne and I. When I visit with her now, she seems content. There is little or no talk of escape. She is filling her time with kindness directed towards other patients. The staff RN asked if Mom had special training in hands-on therapy. She said that she rubs shoulders, pats hands, and comfortingly touches many of the patients. They respond very well to her attention. Sister Mary Mother, my Mom.

Christmas is upon us and we are looking forward to our trip to the Dominican Republic. We will be leaving on the 23rd of December and will not be in town for Christmas. The staff at the care center says that we shouldn't worry about not being there for Mom. They said that she won't know the difference between Christmas and any other day. They are probably right. I hope so.

Tomorrow we will take her to a Christmas performance at the Fine Arts Center. Suzanne's choir will be performing. Jamie will come over also. It should be enjoyable for all.

December 11, 2000

I picked Mom up around 1:00 p.m. on Sunday and we spent the next five hours going from one musical presentation to another. At the end of it all Mom said, "One of the things I live for is music."

We started our adventure attending the lighting of the community Christmas tree. This production was put on by the Florence Hospice Society. They specialize in caring for the old and dying. Parts of the presentation were difficult for Mom. They talked about loss of loved ones and death with dignity. The community chorus sang and a church pastor talked about their work. There was an old Christmas song that was performed "the Heart of Christmas" that took Mom to tears both in this performance and in the later program.

Between performances Mom and I went to the house and she played Christmas songs on the piano. She is playing the piano at the care center. She said that the sound between her piano and that one is quite different. She is unsure which she likes best.

The concert by the Florence Community Concert Band and the Chorus was very good. We sat in the back and had an excellent view. Jamie was able to drive over from Eugene and joined us half way through the performance.

Mom was tired when the concert ended, so I took her back to the care center. She was pleased that the staff was there to greet her and let her tell them all about the music and her adventure.

December 11, 2000

I found Mom walking the halls. "Hi, Mom! How are you?" She said, "I'm pretty good. Things seem to be improving a little." We walked down the long hall where her room was when she first came to the care center. The hall, after a few turns, ends up at a large door and a window that looks over the courtyard. We turned on the way back and passed the music room where the care center keeps a piano. "Would you play for me, Mom?" I asked. She was slow to say yes and did. I sat for forty-five minutes on the bench beside her as she played. It was very nice, and I captured the moment on my video cam.

Hi Sister,

I asked the care center about Mom's reported escape. They said that she has been safely inside the building, and that we shouldn't worry. I trust that they do keep a closer eye on clients like Mom who are looking to escape. Mom did love the day and the music. It's such a pleasure to share the rare good times. I haven't said anything to Mom about our trip. I will probably tell her that I will be gone for a few days and will be back soon. Thanks for reminding me about the gifts for the CNA's. It passed through my mind like the wind through a leafless tree. I will do something today.

I wrote you a bit yesterday about my time with Mom. She has become such a pleasure. The staff is discussing Mom and her treatment Thursday to see if all is being done for her. They seem to feel, from their experience, that the drug you mentioned could causes problems and when the use of it ends the drop is major and often worse than allowing normal degeneration.

James

Hi Sister,

I stood at the end of the hall watched Mom. Her behavior when she is with me is different than when she is relating with the staff. I decided to write an article for our local paper.

James

December 12, 2000

Letter to the Editor,

My father died April 1st of this year. He and my mother shared their home in Yakima, Washington and Dad cared for her. They loved each other. My sister and I did not realize that our mother had Alzheimer's and were unaware of the burden our father had been dealing with for several years. My mother needed continual care, which my sister and I were unable to provide. We began the difficult process of locating a facility or foster home that would meet our mother's needs. After a failed attempt with home care and an unsuccessful placement in a foster home, we admitted Mom to the Siuslaw Care Center in Florence.

Seven months have passed and Mom has gone through many difficult changes while in the care of the center's staff. She has been angry, tearful, confused, defiant, depressed and hopeless. I've been able to visit my mother most every day and have observed the affectionate, patience and skillful attention the entire staff has provided, and I have been very appreciative.

What has warmed my heart and elevated my gratitude of the Care Center most are the Certified Nurse Assistants. Many of them are young men and women. They are the ones that kiss my mother's cheek, that visit with her in her room, and listen to her stories. They are the ones that greet her at the door when I bring her back after an outing, and hug her and help her feel loved and welcome. They are the ones who bring her food when she is hungry, tease her and look at her old pictures of years gone by. They are the ones who help her pick out her clothes and dress her. They are the ones that lighten the guilt I feel not being able to care for her myself.

I watch the CNA's feed and care for patients that have progressed to the point that they are unable to feed themselves, unable to stand or walk, unable to be communicate, unable to do anything but be totally dependant. It comforts me to watch the care of these patients knowing that in months to come my mother will need more help also.

I thank the CNA's and the staff of the Siuslaw Care Center for caring for, and loving, my mother, Virginia Heintz.

December 15, 2000

Today when I pushed the red plunger, which releases the magnets that keep the door secure, I saw a delightful Christmas sight. The door opened to my mother standing with her walker in front of her and a green and red elf hat on her head. She was singing, "Dashing through the Snow" and swinging her hips from one side of her walker to the other. Beside her were two young women with similar hats and another older woman leading the chorus. Ursula, who spends her days in a wheelchair with her head permanently pointed towards the ceiling, was joining in. The singers were surrounded by several patients who were doing what they could to join the celebration.

It seems that Mom has found a way to entertain herself. I have discovered her several times in the music room playing the piano. Some days ago, when I sat beside her and she played for me, I noticed that there was a look of gauntness about her. Her skin was more translucent and draped across her face and hands like a sheet of silk rather than the soft look a light comforter would give. She talks about her skin and is amazed that it will remain pitched like a tent if she pulls it up with her fingers. There is softness in the look of her eyes. For months she has fought the removal of her choices and has been unwilling to submit the management of her life to anyone. The softness in Mom's eyes may come from her believing that the she has control … that she has made choices. Even though she dislikes many aspects of her daily living she is comfortable and mildly entertained.

Today she stands and sings "Glory to the New Born King" and I thank God for the contentment Mom has found and join her in praise.

December 17, 2000

Mom was in her room, in her nightgown, and in a bad mood. She was tossing clothes about and saying naughty words barely below her breath. "Would you like to get out of here for a little while, Mom?" I asked. "Well, what do you think?" she replied and gave me the look one might give a dull child that had just asked the same stupid question for the fourth time. Mom and I took a little drive through Honeyman Park and looked at the different lakes and the beautiful settings. Mom was happy. I could hear her softly humming. The article I submitted to the local paper was printed Saturday. The staff was very pleased that I had such nice things to say about them. They posted the article on the front hall bulletin board where everyone could see, and where Mom could point out what her son had written. When you do the right thing … it feels really good.

January

January 2, 2001

Sweet Sister,

It appears that Mom has entered a new phase of her disease. She is easily angered, has hit a CNA with a coat hanger and is sleeping poorly at night. Both staff and Suzanne, with her family history of Alzheimer's, say that this is normal progression. When I talked with Mom, she said that the CNA deserved to be hit. My, My!!!!

I took Mom out for a drive for several hours today and she loved it. There was lots of sunshine and she talked her head off.

James

Dear Judy,

I sent the below letter to a bunch of old friend addresses I found on Christmas cards in Mom's drawer.

James

January 5, 2001

James Heintz
Florence, Oregon
Dear Roy & Shirley,

I was going through a bunch of Christmas cards that Mom had received and thought that it would be good to share a little information with you about her and how she is doing.

When Dad died in April of 2000 Judy and I were surprised to discover that Dad been caring for Mom in early stages of Alzheimer's. We realized that he had been effectively dealing with many difficult problems and it must have been hard on him.

Judy and I also realized, after consulting with Mom's physician, that she needed a professional environment to keep her safe. After searching many options we moved Mom to Florence, Oregon, where I live. She is a resident of the Siuslaw Care Center.

Judy visits with Mom several times a week by phone and I am able to pop into the care center most every day. There are several family members that call her from time to time and she has received many letters.

At this stage of her Alzheimer's, Mom knows who we all are and remembers family and friends. She does not know what day it is, or if it is morning or night. She has developed a fantasy life that she will talk about in detail. She is often content and occasionally sad and tearful. She wants to be home with Dad at her side and the house filled with us kids. She can walk with the aid of a walker, but has taken to falling lately. Our drives to the beach and through the woods bring her great pleasure. She looks like a tired 82-year-old woman who has lately experienced tough times. Mom can still read a little and enjoys letters and cards.

I thank you for your affection for Mom. She is and has been an exceptional woman and wonderful Mom.

Thanks, James

January 10, 2001

Hi James,

I thought Mom was having a bad time lately. She is back to the tears and confusion of you and Dad during our conversations. She said you remind her of Dad. I can help her for a few minutes but she soon slips back into that sad place. She tries very hard not to cry. I feel so sorry for her.

Love, Judy

January 11, 2001

Sweet Sister,

I remember Mom and Dad talking about when Dad's mom was in her last months and she had disappointment and rejection directed towards Dad. I remember that he suffered under that judgment. Mom's confusion is even more difficult in some ways. She views me as her husband who has left her for another woman. She also feels that she has to be nice when I visit with her even though she feels rejected by me, or I won't come around. I, like you, hate it that Mom is needlessly suffering. I also love you, Judy.

James

January 16, 2001

Lots of time has passed and my reporting on Mom has almost stopped. I was sucking myself dry. Spending time with Mom is like no other experience I have ever had. I experience hopelessness and feel it is my responsibility to be with her and to watch out over her. I find her scattered thoughts to be entertaining and humorous, and dislike her anger when I have disappointed her. The frustration she experiences thinking that I am her husband and living with another woman is so very hard on both of us. She tries to act like everything is OK, but under it all are poorly covered hurts, abandonment and betrayals. She knows that if she allows her feelings to show that I will be uncomfortable with the visits and may not come as often. I hadn't seen her for three days. When I walked into the dining hall she gave me the same look that she used when I was a child. Her look said, "Damn it, why didn't you do what you were told." When I was a kid the look was backed with love. The look I see now exposes her hidden feelings that are laced with scorn. Mom loves me and hates me. In her mind I am what is wrong with her life.

January 18, 2001

Dear Sister,

We visited with Mom late last night. I like to show up at unexpected times to see what kind of treatment she is getting. She was up at 9:30 p.m. and her spirits were good. I was surprised. All is going pretty well here. I hope the same for you.

James

January 18, 2001

"I need to inform you, Mr. Heintz, that your mother struck another patient in the face. She is OK and the woman she hit is OK." I turned off my answer machine and sat in my chair. My God, Mom is punching people out. What does this mean? Will they kick her out of the care center if she becomes violent?

I gave Judy a quick call, and then called the care center to get the details. I was informed that Mom had asked a woman who was sitting in the chair outside of Mom's room to move. It was Mom's place, and she wanted to use it. She asked the woman to move and she didn't. Mom then shook her finger in front of her face and ordered her to move or else. The woman didn't move. Mom then kept her word and rolled up her fist and punched the lady on the end of her nose. An aid was watching and got help from the RN, who asked Mom what had happened. Mom told her in detail and seemed proud of her punch. They tell us that she is on a new drug and that a common side effect is aggressive behavior. I guess we need to change drugs.

January 20, 2001

We sat there holding hands. Mom was eating her dinner with her free hand and we talked and talked. She was happy and telling me about her day's adventures. She had been over to her house and on the way the police had stopped and questioned her about some of the kids that she takes care of. Evidently there were problems in the neighborhood, and there was evidence that some of her kids may have been involved. "For once they weren't looking for me," was her relieved comment. The other residence at the table listened as Mom talked and one, who has both of her feet on the ground, raised her eyebrow a time or two as Mom spun her tails. Thirty minutes into our visit Mom turned to me and with an apologetic look asked, "Are you my husband?" This was a moment that I knew would come, and yet, as I sat beside my mother and looked into her eyes, I realized that she did not know who I was. She knew that I was "her people" but which one was up for grabs. "No, I am not your husband," I said. "Oh, you are my brother?" She asked. "No, Mom, I am not your brother. I am your son, James." "Oh, I am so sorry. Sometimes I can't remember my own name."

January 22, 2001

Hi James,

How is the real estate business going? Will you be spending a lot of time in Eugene with your new business? Are you doing any remodeling at this time? I talked with Mom this morning. She seems more like herself than she has for a couple of weeks. She was OK, not happy, but OK. She did say she misses her family a lot. I talked to a charge nurse yesterday. She said Mom was back on Zoloft at a higher dose. She didn't know why the change had taken place to begin with. We have been having beautiful weather lately. Yesterday, we took the dogs over to the lake for a swim. They had such a good time. It is fun to watch them play. All is OK at the Sacramento front.

Love, Judy

January 23, 2001

Hi Sister,

Today is my first official day back in real estate. I had to retest and take thirty educational hours to reactivate my license. I also have clients who want me to continue my remodel and repair work and are slow to let me off the hook. There will be some over lap and one couple I have done work for wants me to list their home and duplex.

Mom has been pretty good during the last few visits. Like you said in your last letter she is, "OK, not happy, but OK." Did you lose power at your home with the blackouts?

James

January 24, 2001

James,

I keep forgetting to ask you to send me a copy of the article about the Care Center that Mom is in. She was talking about it today.

Love, Judy

January 30, 2001

How do I tell my sister that our mother is acting like a young girl in love. Doc is a new guy who is in a wheelchair and has a foam wrap around his neck. He seems pretty connected to the real world and is thankful for Mom's pushing him up and down the halls. The whole staff is aware that Mom thinks Doc is cool. She has her nails looking great and has lip stick on. She's acting like a junior high kid in love. "Oh, don't you look at me that way," was her comment as I sat beside her and Doc at the dinner table. Doc informed us that tomorrow he would be moving to a foster home. He felt that he wasn't getting the service he needed at the care center. He certainly couldn't have been complaining about the excellent attention he was getting from my mother. Mom said, once she realized that he was going to leave and not return, "I guess I have wasted my time with you." I hope she is not too broken hearted when old Doc rolls out of her life.

January 30, 2001

Hi James,

I was waiting to see if you would mention Mom's new friend! For some time she has been talking about her friend. I am so sorry to hear that he is leaving. She seemed to be so happy. She is so smitten with him. I though life was going to be a little kind to her. Shoot!! Hope all is OK with your family.

Love, Judy

FEBRUARY

February 1, 2001

Hi James,

I am a little bit sore today! A friend and I went cross country skiing yesterday. It had been years since the last time I had been. We had a great day. The weather was great, the snow conditions were great and the company was great. It was a fun time. James how would you feel about giving me a once a week update on Mom? I talk to her every other day and check with the nurses from time to time but you get a one on one feel of how she is doing. If it works for you, it would be great to have the update. Are you pleased to be back in real estate? Is it going well for you? Bye for now

Love, Judy

Dear Sister,

Cross country skiing. It must have been wonderful. I have only done it a few times and found that it was surprisingly difficult. I did love the beautiful country that skiing took me to.

Well let's do a Mom update. Mom is much more loving. This could easily be a byproduct of her med changes. I understand that they upped her Zoloft. Several of the staff nurses have said things like, "She is much more loving, maybe too loving." I have enjoyed her. She is happy to see me and it's OK when it is time for me to leave. I did watch her be firm with Ruby and another lady who wanted Mom to help them. She let them know that she was now going to take time for herself and visit with her son.

Suzanne and I have visited in the evening several nights this week and she has been very sweet to both of us. She has misplaced her glasses again. They will probably show up in a day or two. The last time she lost them on a shelf in another patient's room. She most often walks around without her walker and seems to do OK. If she turns very quickly she will do that toss-the-head-back move. I hope she lands softly the next time she falls. She is eating and hasn't lost more weight. She had her hair curled the other day and looked good. Most often she has on matching sox's and has stories to tell about everything. Very little of her day-to-day reporting is based on reality. I love being around her when she is loving and sweet.

Real estate is going good. I believe that I will have three listings by the end of next week. My office is all fixed up and I have computer software coming that is going to help me do a good job. I have Jamie's cowboy pictures and that old racing car in the office, which gives it a manly look. I think that I am making a good move. I love you sister.

James

February 2, 2001

Dear Judy,

I took Mom to a movie this afternoon, "The Wedding Planner." We watched a little over half of it, and she needed to go home. The staff informed me that Mom has moved into a typical new stage of her Alzheimer's. She has dramatically lowered her inhibition level. She has taken to flashing her breasts in the lobby. They have also found her in the room of the men across the hall. I guess she enjoys rubbing their tired old legs. My, oh my! They said that they are all keeping a close watch on her. Lately she talked a lot about being in love and wanting affection. It's my guess she will be giving us a few more stories to tell. Remember, she was your mother before she was mine.

James

February 3, 2001

Morning James,

Just read your note!! Had to laugh!! Your Mom is a very colorful lady! I talked to her yesterday. Our conversation now makes more sense. Mom was OK, but a little tearful. She said she had gotten into trouble with someone and they had called her a whore. She said she just tries to be nice and look nice, combing her hair and wearing lipstick. She said she had no friends and was so lonely. What a mixed bag! It's funny and sad. Thanks for the note. We are just in the talking stages of making a trip up your way next month. We wanted to visit you, Suzanne, Mom, Bryan and Karrie. Would March be an OK time to visit? Are you working for a real estate company or are you on your own? Is your office in Florence? Got lots of questions. Bye for now.

Love, Judy

February 7, 2001

Hi James,

I just finished talking with Mom. She talked about her glasses being lost. She also said she was wearing glasses now but they weren't hers, so she still doesn't see well. We are having such beautiful weather lately. It is spring in Sacramento. Mag is going up to the cabin for a few days. I have stuff to get done today, so I better get busy. Good Luck with your real estate.

Love, Judy

February 12, 2001

Hi Sis,

The only time during March that we may not be around is in the last week. We look forward to seeing you. I visited for a long time with Mom yesterday. It was a good visit. She was a bit tearful about Dad being unfaithful to her. Today, two years ago, our little brother died. I love you Judy,

James

February 13, 2001

Hi James,

Happy—Happy Valentine's Day! We haven't decided on the exact dates for our trip yet, but we are planning for the first part of March. It will be good to see all of you. This week, Mom has been more clear thinking than she has been for awhile. Sometimes, she sounds like her old self. But, that also means more tears. Have a great Valentine's Day!

Love you, Judy

February 19, 2001

Sweet Sister,

Suzanne & I are going to take Mom out for a hotdog, not a hamburger. She says that she really wants a hotdog. I tried out for a play our community theater is doing. I think that I did OK. Wow! It was a push for me to do this. I think it might be fun.

Little brother

February 19, 2001

Hi James,

I called Mom this afternoon. We weren't on the phone two minutes before she told me about her wedding. She said it might happen tonight. I hope this is a good thing. She is so happy. Maybe she won't need a medication adjustment to improve her life! What is this about you trying out for a play!!! Do we have a budding actor in the family! Bye for now.

Love, Judy

Sweet Sister,

Let's talk about Mom. Last night when I visited with her, she was so tired she could hardly stand. She returned, for the first time in months, to saying, "Where am I going to go when I get out of here?" She looks weak, tired and depressed. She cried several times during the visit. They have changed her back to her old antidepressants, and instead of feeling up and ready to fight, she is down and out. You would think there could be a middle ground. Maybe you could make one of your famous doctor calls and ask for another change in meds. I hate to see her so low. She also has little white growths on her arms, hands and nose. They look like little flat pieces of rice that need flicking off. The nurse said that she would have the doctor look at them and didn't seem concerned. I guess it's just another icky that comes with being old. I don't know why, but Mom has gone from a table dancer to half dead in a week.

The sweet and ever loving little brother loves his sister.

February 22, 2001

Dear Sister,

I met Doc today. He and Mom were in her room knee to knee. She had on a bright flowered top that I haven't seen before. Her eyes were bright and there was color in her cheeks and on her lips. They were leaned over with the tops of their heads almost touching. He was in his wheel chair and she on the edge of her hospital bed. "Hi, Mom! How are you?" I said. She popped up her head and leaned back on her bed with a facial expression that was a mix of embarrassment and surprise. Her hands cover her mouth and she said, "What are you doing here?" I wasn't sure that I was a welcome visitor at that moment. She introduced me to Doc as her son, not her husband, and I shook his hand. He reminded me of pictures of Ernest Hemingway, only beat up. He has a chunk of ear missing the size of a human bite and the ruddy complexion of an outdoorsman. As we talked I learn that he considers himself blind, although he took a picture I offered him for viewing of Inga's granddaughter. He gave me a full update of Mom's medical condition and of the trips that they had taken to the hospital to have one form of treatment or another. He sounded like Dad giving a report on Mom's health. He also told me that Mom had the most beautiful singing voice that he had ever heard. Mom laughed and said, "Oh, you guys. Don't expect too much, you will be disappointed." I asked him if he had listened to her play the piano. He said, "No." He had only heard her sing. He made no moves to leave so Mom and I could visit, so after several minutes of Mom's continuing embarrassment, I said my goodbyes and left. On my way out of the building the staff, with no exceptions, said, "Oh, aren't thy sweet? Don't you just love watching them?"

I am glad to see that she is happy, and I am unsure of my feelings.

James

Dear Sister,

She said they slept together last night and she liked it. She doesn't know his name and he is a nice fellow. He thinks she is the best. She does seem very happy.

The staff at the care center said that he's capable of be a good friend, and that is all. My, oh my!

James

February 27, 2001

Seeing Mom has become such a different experience. It feels much like it did when Dad was alive. She has lost lonesome, and has found contentment and stimulation. She feels alive and is delighted with her feelings. I am happy for her. I feel relieved that I no longer have to be responsible for much of her daily contentment. I do hope that she isn't going to endure another loss.

Her eyes raise and she smiles as I walked through the electronically locked door. "Hi, Honey! What are you doing here so early?" Thinking back I am impressed that she knew it was morning. She and Doc were sitting at the table in the common room in front of the large windows. I could tell that her breakfast was only half eaten and I was not about to be slowed by propriety. "Come on, Mom. You are going for a balloon ride." Over this past year I have developed a much greater appreciation for Mom's adventuresome spirit. With a smile on her face she reached her skin and bone arms towards me so I could help her to her feet. "The Re/Max balloon is giving rides in the parking lot and I am going to take you up." Leaving Mom braced with her hand on Doc's shoulder, I ran down the hall and grabbed an unused wheelchair and returned. With a quick turn and a guided sit down, we were back at the electronic door punching in the escape code and waiving to Doc, who was wishing, "Have fun Virginia! Have fun!" I had spent several hours in the early morning helping the balloonist unpack and inflate his balloon. For the past two years, Re/Max, my real estate company, had hired him to give tethered rides as a promotional gimmick. After a few folks had gone up and down Suzanne, my sweet wife said, "Baby, why don't you go and see if your mother would like to join us?" I was off like a bullet. "See Mom, there it is." The balloon was at the end of its tethers some fifty feet in the air. There was no wind and it was the magical sight that all balloons have in flight. I rolled Mom's chair through the sand and stood her up as the basket touched the ground. The passengers climbed out the back and Mom and I stepped up on the boarding platform together. My good friend, Tom, a mighty big man like myself, helped me lift Mom up and over the padded edge of the basked. She stood there big eyed, as I climbed in beside her. "OK, let's go!" I shouted as the pilot blasted a mass of flame into the balloon's bottom. We lifted off and I delighted in watching Mom's expression as she shifted her view from strait out to down. "Oh my!" were her words as she grabbed my arm and leaned her head against my shoulder. When we reached the end of our tether lines the basket jerked and fear flashed across Mom's face. "It's OK, Mama! Don't be afraid." She was slow to release her death grip, but as we began to descend, I felt the pressure on my arm ease. Landing was easy and with many hands lifting we popped Mom out of the basket and down into her chair, which had been rolled to her side. As quickly as I plucked her from her breakfast table, I took her back. With a quick roll across the parking lot, a push on the electrical door release and a short wheel across the tile floor to her table where Doc and her unfinished breakfast sat, I returned her. "Wasn't that thrilling Mom?" was my question. Her reply was, "Well, I guess it was."

MARCH

March 1, 2001

Hi Sister,

They have decided that Doc and Mom would benefit from a little time apart. Doc doesn't agree. Mom seems OK. I did enjoy my visit with her today without Doc. I guess they were really making a scene. Look forward to seeing you.

Little brother

March 25, 2001

Hi James,

Are you ready for your trip? One last question before you leave. Did you find out what Mom's bra size is? Bras, socks, panties, sweater—that is a lot missing. Are they having laundry problems lately? Hope you have a good trip. Looking forward to seeing you.

Love, Judy

APRIL

April 26, 2001

Two performances are behind me and this afternoon's matinee will bring to a close my adventure into the world of stage acting. Several months ago I was approached by a friend and asked if I would have an interest in performing in the Florence Repertory Theater's presentation of "On Golden Pond." John Flaherty, who has been acting professionally most of his life, encouraged me to give the theater a try. "You will love it, James!" were his words and in some ways he was right. To perform in front of hundreds of people and to feel that I performed well was thrilling. I also agreed to do the play because of encouragement from family members who thought I needed another focus besides Mom. So acting provided not only a thrill, but a diversion, and a good one.

April 28, 2001

Sweet Sister,

Mom is fine. She dropped her glasses and the frames cracked again. She went without for several days and then when I visited and discovered they were broken I repaired them again and she was OK for a while. I made an eye appointment May 15th at 11:30 am with the optometrist.

I haven't been able to visit Mom as often as I did when I was doing contracting. The real estate business seems to demand much more of my time. I do see her every two or three days. Her spirits seem good. She is always with Doc. I have a bit of a bone to pick with the care center staff or some of them anyway. They are shaming Mom. It's a strange process. They will talk about Mom's wanting companionship and how, before Doc, she was being sexual with any resident she could get her hands on. It didn't matter if it was a man or woman. I don't mind Mom doing what ever it is that she does. I do mind information about Mom being shared with the flavor of, "your Mom has been running around here doing the nasty thing with anyone who moves." It takes Mom's dignity away and I don't like that lack of professionalism. It's no big deal. There are a few staff members who don't like Mom and Doc spending time with each other. They dislike it even more that I won't allow them to be kept apart.

The play demanded much time. I did well and got good reviews. I mailed the tape to Jordan and will mail it to you when I get it back. It was hard learning the lines and all the rest of the junk.

Suzanne and I are feeling pretty good. I like riding my bike in the morning and I need to be religious about exercise. I have heard a little more about Doc's daughter moving back to California and taking Doc with her. That will be hard for Mom. I hope the new place opens up about that time. I guess they have plans for excellent activities to stimulate the minds of folks like Mom. Doc is her only stimulation now and that seems to get her into trouble. I love you sister,

James

April 30, 2001

Mom's glasses broke again and I purchased some super glue and put them back together. They held until Mom dropped them again, or that is what was reported to me. Half of the staff had spent two days looking for them and didn't know that someone had turned them into the administrative office. I began my own search, which caused a fuss and was soon informed that they were in a desk drawer awaiting time for someone to take them to the eye doctor for frame repair. I glued them again and believe they will hold until she gets new ones.

Sweet Sister,

I don't know what to tell you or what to think about Mom's bad reputation. It seems that Doc and Mom will sit in the lobby and fondle each other. They don't seem concerned with the lack of privacy and will carry on with or without an audience. I have seen her run her hand inside his shirt and rub his belly.

There is a young man here who shared needles during his drug use days and is dying from hepatitis C. He is the one who has been verbal in his judgment of Mom and talks about her doing the "nasty thing." I have heard some of the staff used similar but milder statements that all carry an attitude of Mom being naughty. I don't know. I don't see why Mom has to be judged by anyone even if she is being sexual. What's with judging her?

She does like to nurture. I will sit beside her and she will rub and rub my leg, sometimes a little higher on my leg than I am comfortable with. I don't believe she means it to be sexual, although affection and sexuality do look a lot alike.

Mom continues to express frustration about Doc, and is always with him. They snap and growl and hug and pat and seem to swing between frustration and enjoyment most all the time. My call is that it is better for Mom to have the relationship than not to.

I hope you have fun at your cabin. The new roof will be a good thing, right?

Mom's hair always looks nice. They are doing a good job. The staff, in general, continues to love Mom and to treat her well. I don't think anyone has shamed her lately or treated her poorly. I do believe that some have judged her harshly. Maybe it is because I refused to allow them to separate Mom and Doc. The ones who judge her are the ones who want them apart. "It will only take a few days of them being apart and she will forget about him," I have heard over and over. I hope this doesn't backfire.

James loves his sister Judy

MAY

May 12, 2001

Hi Sister,

Yesterday I picked Mom up and we took a long drive through some of the beautiful gated communities that we have here. We drove at 20 mph and looked and talked. "Oh! That one would do." "I would take that one." "I wish Johnny was still alive. We could live there." Being with Mom is most always a mix of sadness over her losses and her continuing hope for her future. There is often the "I think I am slipping a little." She often walks around without her walker and does pretty well. She has a little more meat on her bones. Her buddy Doc is most often with her. Pushing his wheel chair is a kind of substitute for using her walker, maybe. They have taken to feeding the two of them at the table in the entry TV room. They both eat better that way. Robin, Doc's daughter, is moving back to California. Doc is staying, at least for a while. His daughter told the staff that he said, "I'm not leaving my woman." She doesn't know how long he will want to stay, but will respect his wishes as long as he is still wishing.

The flowers you sent Mom are beautiful. You are a good daughter. I am going to go outside and mow the lawn. We have been having seventy degree days for a week or so. It's nice and not near as hot as Sacramento. I sold another lot yesterday. Someday I will see some of the green stuff.

The little brother loves his sister

JUNE

June 12, 2001

Hi James,

Are you going to be in town next week? We are talking about driving to Florence. Would a visit be workable with you and Suzanne? I talked to Mom yesterday. She was very upset and lots of tears. It all revolved around Doc?

I've got deck staining to do today. Better get going before it gets too hot. Bye for now.

Love, Judy

June 13, 2001

Sweet Sister,

Yes, come. I visited with them today and they were talking about marriage. Mom kept saying to him "Are you happy now? Doc, are you happy now?" She kept talking with me about the reasons that marriage wasn't a good idea. Mom and Doc seemed OK. I asked them how it would be different if they were married. They didn't know. Mom was not tearful today.

James

June 14, 2001

Hi Sweet Sister,

When I was visiting with Mom & Doc yesterday, I found a letter from Katharine. I read it to them and Mom enjoyed it. As I told you in the little e-mail yesterday, Mom seemed very OK. I hadn't been by in two days and she doesn't seem to notice. She and Doc are locked into a pattern of frustration that I don't think is changeable. Doc, bless his heart, wants to take care of her. So he says,

"Now you had better get off your feet and rest a little. Watch out, there is a spot of water on the floor. Now don't sit too close to the window, you will catch a cold from the draft." This is his was of being loving, however, Mom doesn't want him to do anything but tell her she is pretty and has a beautiful singing voice.

My business is starting to make money. I am even with most of my expenses and am starting to make a little. We look forward to seeing you. Will you be here next week? What day? Coming on a Monday would be fine. We just have soup and sit around and talk about different religious views of different topics. It would be great to have you be a part of that.

I was saying my morning prayers yesterday and was thinking about Dad's funeral at the church. I was thinking about his coffin being carried by his grand-children and you and I walking into the church behind them. The memory and missing Dad touched me. I cried for a while. I miss him. I miss Steve. My life is very full and God has blessed me over and over, and yet I do have holes that I can't fill with all the good in my life. I love you Sister.

James

Judy and I have been hearing about the opening of a new facility named Elderberry Square that will specialize in the care of Alzheimer's patients. We understand that it will feel more like a home and not have the nursing home atmosphere. We are working to get Mom on their new client list and are hopeful. Perhaps a change in places will also take care of the multiple concerns that Judy and I have over Mom's relationship with Doc. On the one hand, we are happy that she feels loved and cared for, like she was for the sixty-two years that she and my dad were married; on the other, neither she nor Doc are mentally fit to make decisions about marriage. So many ramifications to consider.

June 27, 2001

Sweet Sister,

She is tired and seems OK in the balance area. I talked with the staff about the move and they were in agreement that the move should be made without Doc. They feel that the additional stimulation will shortly override Mom's missing Doc. I hope we are making the best decision.

James

July

July7, 2001

Among the many people who I was able to reconnect with during my mom's illness was my brother's first wife, Shirley. She had attended my brother's funeral in 1999, then my father's in 2000. After not having contact for some twenty years, it was comforting to talk to her about Mom. Shirley and Steve had started dating in high school, so Shirley has been a part of our family since girlhood, and has known and loved my mom for years.

Dear Shirley,

I was rolling through my address book and found your address and thought that you might like to have a little update on Mom. She has lived for the past year in the Siuslaw Care Center in Florence, and had slowly adjusted and found a level of peace in her life. She is confused about many things and yet keeps all of us that she has loved pretty clear. She can't tell you what year it is, or where she lives, and can tell you all about her high school boy friends, and all her grand children. Speaking of grandchildren, I am now a grandpa. Jamie had a son last week. They named him Skylar, and he's a real beauty. He has lots of long dark hair and I believe I heard him say, "Hi Grandpa," but I am not sure.

Back to Mom. She has pretty good health and walks with a walker. I thought she would die after Dad's death, but she didn't and seems stronger every day. She has a guy friend in the care center who she spends time holding hands and smooching with. She calls him John and his name is Doc. We have an opportunity to move her to a new facility here which will open in a few weeks. It is designed to deal with folks who have Alzheimer and should be more stimulating than the place she is now.

Suzanne and I are well. I am selling real estate again with Re/Max and doing OK after a slow start this spring. My old body gave out on the contracting work and I will probably be working until I am seventy, if I live that long, so I wanted a profession that was a little less demanding physically. I hope this note finds you well. I don't have Jackie's e-mail address. I would love to have it. I hope to hear from you soon.

James

We discovered that Mom was on the eligibility list for Elderberry but wouldn't be admitted as soon as we had hoped, due to delays in the completion of the facility and all the necessary inspections and licensure procedures required before they can accept patients.

July 26, 2001

Hi James,

Well, now that Mom is going to stay at the care center for a few more weeks, there is the problem of Doc. Do you think that we should ask the care center to see if they can give Mom more time away from Doc, and maybe not have them eat together? Do you think it would be worth a try to see if Mom and Doc would do better away from each other? I am concerned about Mom. She seems, from what I am hearing, to be getting more and more depressed over the relationship. She tells me that she does not want to be around Doc, but she is so lonely. So, is she worse being lonely or being around Doc? At this point in time I am beginning to think being around Doc is giving her more pain than pleasure. The staff at the care center can now say, "I told you so!" What do you think? Bye for now!

Love, Judy

Jul 27, 2001

Sweet Sister,

Yes, I think we need to work on it. I don't know how successful it will be moving Mom to Elderberry Square, and I am unsure what the best path is. I will talk with the care center staff this weekend and see what they think. I will keep you posted.

The sweet little brother.

10

WE MOVED MOM TO ELDERBERRY SQUARE

September 28, 2001

Hi James,

I rescheduled Mom's doctor's appointment. Will Oct. 26th, 3:00 p.m. work? I talked to Mom and Don, the manager of Elderberry Square. Mom gave the phone to him while he was standing beside her and we had a visit. He said that they have been slow getting a music program set up, but it will be falling into place soon. I told him the two complaints I hear from Mom are that she is lonely and bored. Hopefully the two outings a week we have set up with the companionship service will be helpful for her. Did I tell you that it will be about $200.00 a month? If it helps to make Mom's life better, I think it is well worth it, don't you? Mom's mind seemed much clearer than it has been. Don said that it was a very good thing if Mom had her own piano. I thought you would be glad to hear that. Let me know if the new doctor's appointment works with your schedule. Bye for now.

Love, Judy

Dear Judy,

I had the piano moved to Elderberry Square. I hope she enjoys it. When she first sat down at the keyboard, she seemed confused. I'm not sure she knows that it is her piano. Mom does seem to be doing well in some ways. I don't think her color and physical mobility are too hot. At times she doesn't track real well, but does seem a bit happier these last few days. The appointed date for the doctor's visit looks good for now. I don't know what is so hard about calling a few folks and asking them to come in and do a bit of music. I think I could, with no information available now, call around and get names and set up a system in a few hours. Maybe I will offer to do that.

James

October

October 3, 2001

Hi Sister,

I saw Mom the other day, after not being by for four days, and she was great. She did say "Seems like I haven't seen you for a day or two." We are off on our Mexico trip Saturday and will be back the following Sunday. Love ya,

Oh! The other day when I went in to Elderberry Square there was an old couple doing a church service and Mom was singing her heart out. It was good. That was probably part of why she was in a good mood.

James

October 16, 2001

I have sent out Mom's new address to some not all. I am unsure who. Oh well.

October 17, 2001

The change from Siuslaw Care Center to Elderberry Square didn't go as smoothly as Judy and I had wanted. Their program was new and they weren't able to offer the services we desired as quickly as we wanted. There were also difficulties with Mom's medication. The staff working the night shift would give Mom meds to calm her and I would find her slumped over in her wheel chair the next day unable to sit up or keep her mouth shut. They didn't know her well enough to know that a Tootsie Roll Pop was the best medicine when she was anxious and needed to be calmed.

Not one to let things be left undone, I felt compelled to voice my concerns and establish myself as a family member who was tracking the care of my mom and not acquiescing about services. I wrote a letter, at the risk of being a pain in the…. Time and again, Judy and I had to advocate for Mom. We had to stand up for her and the person she had been in order to get the needs of the person she is now met. We want her to enjoy the best health and happiness possible. Mom has had her med's adjusted in the past to assist her with anger, frustration, anxiety, depression etc. I find it interesting that the adjustment to a new facility is a whole family process, not just a personal one for Mom.

NOVEMBER

November 6, 2001

Good Morning James,

I forgot to give you a little more information I got from Jackie (the Senior Services Case Manager who has helped us so much). Perhaps you already know. They do keep a medical chart for all of the patients at Elderberry. My understanding is that they make entries regularly—I don't know about daily. You have the right to look at Mom's chart anytime you wish. I thought it might be interesting to see what they wrote about the days that Mom seemed overdosed. Also would you mind asking the doctor how much weight Mom has lost since she has been at Elderberry Square. She looks good, but Chris said that she only wants to eat desserts. It is not going to be good if she continues to lose weight. Also, would you ask about the meds that make her so drugged. I am curious to see what he has to say. Even if Mom was given the maximum dose, it still should not have been so strong that it knocks her out. I am a pain in the butt, aren't I? I come to visit and all the information that is new to me is old information to you. How did your meeting go last night? Mag wants to know what kind of soup you had! Hope you sell a house today.

Love, Judy

November 6, 2001

Sweet Sister,

The soup was pumpkin and green pepper. It was sweet and mild. Every one liked it. It was a little too bland for me. I like the soups spicy. I will find out the name of the med Mom is on and how much weight she has lost.

Love you, James

As the months went by and the persistent care of Mom became assimilated into my daily life, I came to terms with many things and found daily visits and emails less necessary. Days would pass, the irregularity of Mom's moods and the ups and downs of her health were a given.

November 17, 2001

Dear Sister,

I am working so very hard to make my real estate business a success and am doing pretty well for my first year.

James

DECEMBER

In an attempt to give Mom all the happiness of the holiday season, Suzanne and I arranged a big Christmas party at our house, inviting friends and family. Decorations included some of Mom's own decorations from Christmases past. We wondered if she would notice.

December 24, 2001

Hi Judy,

Sorry about the party starting just as we tried to have our phone visit. Mom didn't last long at the party. Around 6:00 p.m. she said that she was tired, so I took her back to Elderberry Square. She was anxious to see Rob, her new guy friend. She went directly to him and told him how much she had missed him and gave him a big kiss. Here we go again.

She had a pretty good time with us. She did like your gifts. I could tell. She cries a lot at times like this. All the old memories flood in and take her over. I asked her if she thought it would be better to forget the holidays and she said, "No, we have to do something." When I arrived at Elderberry to pick her up, she thought I was Dad and called me John. She was very happy to see me and took my hat off to show Rob my hairless head. She was surprised to find hair. The little I have is much more than Dad had. I liked it that she was thinking of Dad, and appreciated that she is becoming a bit more confused as each month passes.

Judy, Mom does seem very happy around Rob, and he does seem to treat her well? After the problems that ended her relationship with Doc, I do feel a little anxious. Rob is also very friendly with other women. I think this is where the rub comes. Mom doesn't like him to call other women sweetheart and such. All said and done, I think, at this time, that he is far more of a plus in Mom's life than a minus. I think!

Have a wonderful holiday with Mag and Lee. Every year, my celebration of Christmas changes. I love you Judy and wish every good for you and those you love, which, thank God, includes me.

Little brother James

December 25, 2001

Sweet Sister,

Mom seems to have high times and low times, doesn't she? There have been many times lately when I have visited her that she has seemed happier than normal, with very few sad times. We thank you for your gifts. Your sugar free goodies were good. I am always surprised when they are. Christmas with Jamie and Skylar was great. We stayed over Christmas Eve and had two wonderful days. I went golfing nine holes with Jason. I loved it. On one par three hole, I swacked it good and it landed by the hole, only two feet away. Everyone was impressed. I have a set of clubs and I think that I may golf a bit. Suzanne rode her bike over to my office to bring me lunch. She fell and broke her arm. It's broken in the elbow. She is in a bit of pain, and sad that all she can do for her vacation is watch TV. I will write again soon.

James

December 26, 2001

Dear James,

Thank you for the nice email. How was your Christmas? I called Mom yesterday. She only talked for about five minutes. She asked me to call her back because she wasn't feeling well. I gathered she was feeling sad. It seems this Christmas was more sad for her than last year. Thank you and Suzanne for the gifts. The goodies were delicious. Needless to say, they are already gone. The honey and jelly are good, too. The scented table protector is nice. The highlight of Mag's day was the Whoopee cushion! We got some good laughs out of that one. I am sure there will be more!

Love you, Judy

JANUARY

January 3, 2002

Dear Elderberry Square,

Several months ago when I had the family piano moved to Elderberry Square, I had the fantasy that Mom would spend many hours each day pleasing herself and others with her music. I had also hoped it would be used by others in the musical programs that were being developed.

I have been very disappointed that Mom didn't take to her piano. She played it a little at first, but now she doesn't even know that it is hers, and has no interest in it. It also appears that it is not an important part of your musical program, and is probably more in the way than an asset.

I love Mom's piano and have missed it in my home. It reminds me of the wonderful sounds she would make when the house chores were done and she had a few moments to herself.

With your approval I would like to have my movers pick it up and return it to my home.

Thanks for understanding,

James Heintz

January 9, 2002

Hi Sister,

I wrote Elderberry Square a letter and said that Mom wasn't using the piano and to my knowledge no one else was. The patients' wheelchairs are grinding the finish off the legs and the sides. Mom had kept it scratch free, and it makes me sad to see it so beat up. They responded by telling me that Mom plays it often, and they do use it when music presentations are scheduled. I said OK. I will leave it there.

James

January 9, 2002

Hi James,

I forgot to tell you last night that Betty said they are using the piano on Wednesdays. I don't know what your plans for the piano are at this point in time, but I thought you might like to know that it is being used. Have a good day!

Love, Judy

January 15, 2002

He is just sitting there watching TV. He looks pretty dapper considering he is one of the patients at a care facility. His skin has a hearty glow. He looks healthier that anyone else in the room including the staff. For a while he had a beard that gave him a sinister look. Now he has trimmed it down to a full white, mustache. He looks like he could give a damn about someone. His giving a damn about someone is why I am writing this little piece. An old woman is sitting with her head on his shoulder, her eyes closed and her hand lying on the inside of his leg. This old woman was married for over fifty years to the same man. She raised three kids and devoted her life to her husband and children. Her social life was filled with family, homemaking and friendships with other women living in her neighborhood. Her name is Virginia and I call her Mom. Mom can't remember Rob's name and he doesn't seem to care. "Hi, Mom! How are you doing?" She opens her eyes and smiles. "Hi, Honey. How are you? What have you been doing today?"

We move into our little visiting routine, as I sit in the empty spot beside them on the couch. She places her other hand on my leg and asks Rob if he remembers me? "Sure! He is your son, James." Rob does real well with the first two sentences and then moves into another world of processing that I am not a part of. He speaks of the trip he and Mom had taken to Hawaii before lunch. Mom is able to join Rob in the place where well minds can't go. They can talk about the great adventures they had that day and the amazing sights they saw. It's like two kids holding hands and spinning across a field of delusion. They seem happy.

It is time for another general letter to friends and family to fill them in on Mom's condition. I haven't sent an update for a long time. Here is what I had to say, nearly two years after the beginning of this roller coaster of her life began.

Dear Family,

Let me tell you how Mom is doing! She's pretty good. She can walk and often doesn't. She got herself a new wheelchair, and seems to prefer rolling around in it instead of using her feet. I took off the footplates to give her full kicking power in forward or reverse. She most often knows me. One day, after I had visited with her for a while, she said, "You are my blood, aren't you?" She can be visiting with me, take a break to go to the bathroom, come out and say, "Oh! Hi James! When did you come by?" Most often when I visit, I will find her sitting at the dining room table with her friend, Rob. Rob is very nice to Mom and they hold hands and talk like old married people. She often calls him John or "that fellow." They also tell great stories about their day's adventure. Trips to San Francisco or Sacramento are normal. They look at each other and fill in the details to any question I may ask, and are most always in agreement. It is like participating in Story Telling 101, and these two deserve A+'s.

Looking at Mom would probably surprise you a little. She is old, very slow in movement, lots of skin on old bones, her face is thin, and she talks of her hands looking like they belong on an "old woman." Her smile, which I get to see lots of, is the same and her eyes still sparkle. I don't think her vision is great, and yet she could read a small word in the newspaper the other day. I was impressed. Her body parts seem to be working and she is dressed clean, pressed and well. Her sox always match, and her shoes are on the right feet. If I miss seeing her for a few days, she is OK with that. She doesn't seem to notice. She likes her room, but spends most of her time in the dining room with Rob. She has her piano in the dining room and, with a little encouragement, she plays. Sounds pretty good. After she gets warmed up, she will close her eyes and play and play. I have often wondered what she is thinking as her fingers cross the keys and fill the room with her music. Others, who come to entertain the old folks, use Mom's piano. Judy and I like that. Her world is pretty small now. All the people she loved are around her in memory, and not a part of her daily life. Lately she has been talking a lot about her mom and dad and her life in Naches. When she remembers that they have died, she cries. Her daily life is filled with a caring staff, who do enjoy her and her spicy personality, her friend Rob, myself, with visits from Judy and Mag, and an occasional visits from Jamie, and her son Sky. She loves her great grandson! It's fun to watch her hold him and make him smile. She does enjoy the phone calls she receives and the letters that are read to her. Mom told me the other day that she is always planning for her future. "What would you have if you couldn't plan for a better tomorrow?" she has often asked me.

Thanks,

James Heintz

January 17, 2002

Hi Sister,

All is pretty good. My business is hard sometimes. I work and work and often it is for naught. Working for naught is not very good pay. I do expect to have some good things happen soon. I will be working on Mom's stuff later today. I will mail it to you for your thoughts. I heard also that Betty didn't take Mom out. I guess Mom can get pissed and unwilling to do much that they would like to see. I did her nails yesterday and we had a good visit. I guess the hair deal there didn't come about. We need Betty to take Mom out. I be loving you.

James

January 26, 2002

Sweet Sister,

I love you.

James

FEBRUARY
MARCH
APRIL

Sometimes taking the time to talk about or record Mom's unchanging world doesn't happen. Visit after visit seems the same. It's like we are in God's little waiting room, and yesterday, today and tomorrow are one.

April 5, 2002

Hi James,

Glad to hear you are busy and doing well. I have a few questions, so I thought email might work better for you. How does Mom's perm look? She told me that she didn't need a perm! Has the dentist's office given you a call yet? On my calendar I have Mom scheduled for a complete physical on April the 19th. How does that work for you? Bye for now.

Love, Judy

Hi sister,

Thanks for the e-mail. Mom's dental plate is in and I have called to set an appointment for her to get it. They have not returned my message on their machine, so I don't know when. Her hair looks good. It doesn't look like a perm, and it doesn't smell like a perm. I don't think it is a perm, and it looks good. It is pretty short in back and on the sides. She seemed OK. The complete physical on April 19th should be OK. What time of day? I am sorry that we have missed each other on the phone. The little and younger brother loves his old, big sister.

James

MAY

May 23, 2002

Hi Sister,

The last couple of days have been Mom and the doctor days. Yesterday she had her girl check-up and the physician's assistant thought that it would be better if she checked Mom out every six weeks rather than every three months. On Tuesday we had the mammogram. For both visits she was in good spirits.

When I go to Elderberry to pick her up, I always find her with Rob. Sometimes they are in the dining room, often in his room, and yesterday her room. She was asleep on her bed and he was in her new chair watching over her. When you called the other day to inform me that Mom and Rob were married I was tickled. Mom now drops her voice, leans towards me and whispers in my ear "We're married you know. I don't know when it happened but he, you know, the man who keeps changing his name, says so." She will then give me that look that one might expect to see on the face of a sixteen year girl who was just told she was loved by the most handsome and popular boy in school. It's funny how at times I feel Mom's life has no little meaning, and then she gets that sixteen-year-old look, and I have to appreciate that there are moments when she is delighted. What more can anyone ask for?

James

There's a bony fist shaking in my face. A foot behind it my mother's angry face is crunched and her words strike through her lips with a "Do you know what I want to do to you guys for putting me in here?"

Its Memorial Day weekend, and I haven't found myself taking the time I should to visit with Mom. I am not sure that saying "I should" is correct. It just seems like I should, but I am not highly motivated to visit. She is content with Rob. If he is there, she doesn't seem to have any great needs. It is so much like her life with Dad. I feel kind of off the hook and not responsible. Anyway, I will try to visit tomorrow. She is always happy to see me. They act like I am the good son dropping by for a little visit.

I love looking in Mom's eyes. Even in her confused state, I see her love for me. I, in the strangest way, miss being the one she depends upon. I guess I am her kid again. God blesses us in strange and unexpected ways.

JUNE
JULY
AUGUST
SEPTEMBER

October 19, 2002

Dear Friends and Family,

Months have passed and I have not placed a word on paper to record the days of my Mother's life. When we reversed rolls, my Mother and myself, I found my sister and I had responsibility for her. In the past, the words I wrote about that reversal helped me identify, understand and deal with my new feelings. I felt needed by her, and found a degree of fulfillment and satisfaction in being there to support her. The changes seemed endless for Mom, and contentment was not hers to be had. After foster-care, and the Siuslaw Care Center, we moved her to Elderberry Square, a new facility that specializes in Alzheimer's patients. It was there that she found some middle ground, something that looked a little bit like contentment. She also found an old guy, named Rob, who became her friend. They kept each other company, as their minds lost track of themselves. They tell stories of the far away places they just visited together, and the ones they saw jointly when they were young.

Almost a year had passed at Elderberry Square when, about a month ago, Mom had pain. Her lower gut, hip and back seemed to be the source of the problem, yet the medical tests revealed nothing. Judy and I pushed the medical system, and pushed it again, in our attempts to find an answer and relief for Mom. Pain had become a blanket she was under, and it wasn't allowing itself to be pulled away as it confined her to bed and devoured her energy. She is in her bed today. She is comfortable until it is time for her next pain pill, or she is moved. We still don't know why she hurts. She can't talk and be understood. Her meds keep her eyes half closed, and her mouth can't quite form the words she wants to share.

Tomorrow they are moving Rob to the new building next door. The administrator at Elderberry Square think there will be fewer problems between the clients if they have one building for the women and the other for men. Rob & Mom won't be seeing each other anymore. Tuesday we will visit a chiropractic physician. Judy and I have run out of options and have our hopes stacked on the chiropractor's skill. I have asked Mom if it was OK to read prayers to her and for her. She didn't answer, but closed her eyes until I was done.

James Heintz

October 29, 2002

Suzanne and I are going to Haifa, Israel on our Baha'i pilgrimage, and we're going to be gone for twelve days. It was hard to leave, knowing that Mom was not well and in great pain. I tried to get all Mom's affairs in order before I left.

Dear Sister,

I spent some time today visiting with the Burns's Riverside Chapel. As I said, I didn't want to leave town and have Mom die and leave you with all the details. Here is what I arranged, and it is all subject to change. The coffins, nicer ones, cost between $1,800 and $3,500. I am sure we could spend much more than that if we wanted. Most of them are big metal or metallic like boxes and they are full of crumpled, accordion-like fabric. The one I liked best was an all wood box. It was simple in design with no metal used. The handrails and hinges were all wood. It had a domed top and had a clean modern look. The one I saw had dark wood finish with white satin interior and was tailored. Although it is strange to say, it looks quite comfortable. Mr. Burns said that he can order it in a lighter wood with a light blue lining. I would be proud to have people see us burying Mom in this coffin.

If Mom dies while I am gone, they will pick her body up at Elderberry Square and take it to the Funeral Home. There they will wash her body, they always do that, and wrap it in cotton sheets, which would please me most, or dress her in an outfit if we wanted. He said that they would not have to embalm her. This pleased me, in that I don't like the idea of Mom's body being drained of her blood and pumped full of formaldehyde. It is sad enough that I wouldn't be there to say prayers as her body was washed. They would then place her in the coffin and transport her to Yakima. He said that they would call Yakima today to find out everything they need to do for internment. The family would then have a graveside service. I would ask family to read things that they thought Mom would like, and to say things that they would like to say. Simple, just the way I think Mom would want it.

Costs: Internment would be $500 to $1,000. They will have that final figure in a day or two, after talking with Yakima. The Funeral Home service for pick up, washing, death certificate, arrangements would be $1,045. The transport would be less than $500.00. The coffin I liked was $1,800. He said that he may be able to reduce that by $200. He would check with the owner of the Chapel. The Burns's Chapel would pay Yakima for their charges and present us with one bill from them. So, not considering flowers and stuff, it will run around $4,000. You and Mag can go directly to Yakima and know that Mom's body will be treated with great respect.

I gave Mr. Burns your number, and he may call you if he needs more information. I will inform Elderberry Square of our set up with Burns. It could work out that you would be here and it may be a comfort for you to know that everything was arranged. I do not know about, as Mom would say, the "Oh Bitch." If you supply me with all the information about Mom, I don't know any of the important dates, I will write up something for the Yakima paper and the Burns people would take care of it when the time came. I also thought that picture that was the other side of the one we used for Dad, the one with Mom in her wedding suit and that cute hat, would be good. If you disagree with any of this and want something different, let's talk and figure out another answer. You and I get to make all the decisions. I want it to be right for you, as well as for myself. This is difficult stuff.

The brother deeply loves his sister and our Mother.

Of course, Mom didn't die while I was in Israel. I got home and eagerly went to see her. She was much as she had been … remarkably the same.

November

November 14, 2002

October was not a good month for my Mother. It wasn't a good month for me either. Gloom and doom seem to be my filter for viewing Mom's life. Being hopeful about her tomorrows has been difficult for me. When Dad died and Mom's poor health became obvious to my sister and myself, I gave up hope for her. I have been giving up on her for a couple of years now. Last month something went wrong. She led us to believe it was in her lower gut or possibly her back. We never knew for sure, and don't know now. The pain just passed. It just went away. Why? She was slow in regaining her stamina, and is still in the wheelchair. What is back is her ability to get angry. Once again, she wants to move home to Yakima. It seems that the closer she is connected to the real world, the greater is her desire to escape her current circumstances. When she had her old guy buddy, Rob, she felt at home. Now that he has been removed from her life, she is alone in a house filled with women. Mom doesn't really like women.

One of the other patients doesn't like Mom. Last week she took her tennis shoe covered foot and kicked Mom in the leg. The parchment like skin stretched across the bones of Mom's legs tore. The staff patched her up and Mom didn't seem to know the difference. She knows the difference today. Her leg is twice the size of the other and her foot looks like a surgeon's glove blown up to entertain a child. The veins and swollen tissue are pushed to the surface and are red and angry. Yesterday we drove to the doctor for more antibiotics. Between the bladder infections and infections from other injuries, she has processed a backpack of antibiotics. They probably don't do much anymore.

November 19, 2002

As I watch Mom's tired, bruised body slouch in her wheelchair, I again think about her impending death. It is strange how "impending" can be such a huge word. From my perspective, this figure in the chair looked so different from the Mom I had known all my life, and so debilitated, it was hard for me to imagine that she could go on living for very long at all. I decided to write up the obituary I had mentioned to Judy before my trip to Israel.

James Heintz
Florence, Oregon 97439

Information needed for a press release in the Yakima, Washington Newspaper following the death of Virginia P. Heintz

Virginia was born in Richland, Oregon on March 13, 1919. She was the first of three children born to Irene Potter and Fred Curtis McDougall. When Virginia was a small child, her father moved the family to Naches, Washington. She grew up in that small farming community and attended local schools until she graduated from Naches High School.

In 1938 she met Johnny Heintz, who became her husband on July 9, 1939. They, after living in several small northwest communities, settled in Yakima, Washington, where they lived together as husband and wife for 61 years. Three children filled their home and hearts. Judy Myre of Sacramento,

California, James Heintz of Florence, Oregon, and Steve Heintz of Yakima, who died several years ago.

Virginia was a woman devoted to her children. She attended to their every need when they were small, and was delighted with their friendships as adults. She loved her music, gardens and homes. Throughout her life she pleased herself by spending time with friends and family, playing her piano, making her home beautiful and admiring beauty created by others. Virginia had seven grandchildren and four great grandchildren who brought her great pleasure.

Following the death of her husband, Virginia moved to Florence, Oregon where she lived until her death 00/00/00. Her death was age related. Virginia's body will be placed to rest in the Terrace Heights Memorial Gardens in Yakima, Washington at 0:00 p.m. month/day/year.

DECEMBER

December 2, 2002

Mama is back. She is old and low on fuel. Lately she has run into hard luck with lots of incapaciting back pain. The source of the pain seemed to elude the medical profession. I wonder if that happens more often when people are old and look to be only moments from their coffin. The recommended treatment was pain pills, which have always put Mom on her rear and leave her with the speech pattern of the demented.

December 12, 2002

Greetings Family and Friends,

I wanted to draft this note for all of you who have concerns about Mom and her health. When I last wrote Mom was in a spiral of pain that seemed hopeless. Judy and I were beside ourselves attempting to find a treatment that would give her relief. I think that the local medical community was a bit anxious when they heard that it was Judy or me on the line. We pushed and pushed, with no success. When we were ready to set traditional treatment aside and roll Mom to a chiropractor, she got better. Her pain left as it came, within days.

We also had to deal with the care center's decision to separate the men from the women. Mom had a friend who watched out for her and was there to hold her hand most all the time. When they moved him, she was upside down in her six weeks of pain and didn't noticed.

Today she is better than she has been in months. There is another client who Mom has disliked from the day she joined the facility. This gal has kicked Mom three times now, removing long strips of skin from her shins. Twice Mom's legs became infected and there was so much swelling that she couldn't wear her shoes. The last attack occurred a few days ago and we have been informed that its slipper time for Little Miss Kicker.

Mom is happy to visit and is in good spirits. She does recognize me, though sometimes is a little slow in that process. She is often confused with moments of astonishing clarity. Talking about old friends and family is good for her and daily occurrences often escape her memory.

With the removal of the men from her facility she finds herself thinking about Dad and talking about him. Sometimes she cries; other times she is content, and the talks easily. I like it when she smiles at her memory of him and the things they did together.

I will keep you all posted as Mom goes through these days of her life that are such an interesting mix of loss, confusion and occasional contentment, maybe even moments of happiness.

James

JANUARY

January 27, 2003

The call back was not what I wanted to hear. I was upset again and I had put Judy on the problem. Earlier in the day I had visited with Mom and had found her under the influence of her anti-anxiety drug. She was slumped to one side in her wheelchair and when I knelt down in front of her and gave her my best smile I didn't get anything back. Her expression was the same as many of her fellow patients, loose and without expression. "Hi, Mama!" The pause was long and slowly the smile, that does not necessary mean recognition, forced its way onto her face. If they leave her alone and don't drug her, my visits have been pretty good. She isn't connected to the happenings of the world and certainly could not talk about the fears we are experiencing as our country is posed for war. She doesn't know the name of anyone around her and now often mixes me up with my dead Uncle Don. What she can do is smile, laugh and talk about her past. We like to do that, when I chip a little time out of my workday, and visit with her. We can have a handful of good visits, then I will have a day like today. "When was Mom last medicated, and what did you give her?" It's my immediate question and the staff is quick to lead me to her medical chart. Today I discovered that for the past three days, just after dinner, she had been given meds that put her on her butt. I feel badly that so many days have passed without my checking on her. "What has been going on that has warranted her being medicated at the same time three days in a row. The staff member that was looking at the chart didn't know, but promised me she would check into it. I'm not looking to find fault with the staff. I am concerned that some unqualified employee, who doesn't want to deal with a little evening anxiety, is choosing to medicate Mom to lighten their evening's workload.

My visits are most often midday and she is enjoyable, if is she isn't doped up. The report Judy gave me that was disappointing is that Mom is a bit out of hand. They talk of agitation with other patients, paranoid, angry and difficult to work with. I have seen these behaviors before. I don't want Mom to be in that state and have always believed that if folks would take a little time and entertain and distract her, the meds wouldn't be necessary, and I could have the sweet visits with my Mom that have become precious. Today, when I stood to leave, hoisting myself out of a chair in the dining room, I discovered that my backside was sopping wet with another mother's urine.

FEBRUARY

February 11, 2003

"It's a fake, Honey. I do it every day," were Mom's words as she began to cry. Our visit had started with her rolling down the hall in her chair and softly smiling when I leaned over her shoulder and kissed her cheek. "It's been a while. How did you find me?" She often, on her good days, starts our visit this way. I am struck by the poignancy of her remark. Because she is lost, she wonders how I can find her. I know that she recognizes me as family, and I am not sure that she is able to do much more than that. We had talked a little and something I said washed her into talking about her day-to-day living and all the effort she puts out to appear OK. Letting her spend time in tears doesn't change anything, so I quickly directed her attention to the birds that were on the fence outside the window. She reentered her world of fake as she does every day.

February 19, 2003

Hi James,

Would it be OK if we arrived at your place March eleventh and departed the fourteenth? We can have a little birthday party for Mom! Hope your visit with the doctor and Mom went well.

Judy

Hi Sister,

The Doctor visit is today at 4:15 pm. The 11th, 12th, 13th, and 14th sound great. We look forward to having you back in town. Mom is being fed now. On her own, she gets most of her food on the floor and her lap. She isn't sitting up well in her chair, but the staff reports that she is not on any mood altering meds. She smiles, talks a little and isn't real well connected. She does not seem sad. Maybe another stroke? I don't know.

James

February 25, 2003

My niece, Erica, lives in Yakima with her new husband, Josh. She spent lots of time with Grandma & Grandpa Heintz as a little girl, and finds it hard to imagine her grandmother in this current state, so different from the Grandma she remembers. She wrote me a concerned email, asking about Mom. I responded:

Hi Erica,

I am always delighted when my incoming mail pops up with your name. I am glad that you and Josh are doing well. Your grandmother looks like she belongs in an old folk's home. For a long time I would walk in and see her dressed well, not a stain on her clothing, hair just right and all the stuff we have always associated with Mom. Now, she slumps way over to one side of her wheelchair. They stuff a sofa cushion between her ribs and the arms of the chair so she won't bruise herself. We keep her hair pretty short so that messed or not, it looks OK. She can't find her mouth when she eats, and ends up with lots of her food on her and on the floor. When I sit her up, she feels like I am pushing her over and returns to her hanging position. Her speech in confused. Getting a full, logical sentence out of her is hard. Her voice also fades at the ends of sentences, so it is difficult to hear her. She is very thin. When you talk to her, after she takes a few moments to recognize you, you get the smile. Like you, she wants to buy a beautiful home and loves to drive through neighborhoods picking out her future favorite. Some times I think that she must be getting close to the end, and then she gets better and starts rolling down the halls again. The place she lives is very clean and home like. The support staff is excellent. Judy and I are pleased with the service they give Mom. Love,

Uncle James

MARCH

March 16, 2003

Judy and Mag are here for Mom's birthday. She is 84 today. Judy has procured a cake, ice cream, birthday hats, and balloons for a party at Elderberry Square. As Judy & Suzanne set up the festivities, several of the residents gather around in anticipation of something exciting. Mom is the queen of the evening, smiling and laughing and loving being the center of attention. She ceremoniously blows out her candles (with help from others). Judy & Suzanne cut the cake and serve plates of cake & ice cream to those gathered. One gentlemen in a wheel chair points to a spoon and says, "Can I have … uh … that … uh …" He can't remember the word. Suzanne hands him a spoon and he begins to eat. After dessert, the same man pulls a harmonica out of his shirt pocket and begins to play. We join in with song as he plays and plays old songs from the 20's, 30's, 40's. Then Mom is at the piano and she plays and plays, one melody after another, with little transitional musical phrases between. The evening is grand! But the mystery! Here are these people who don't know where they are or who they are with or even "spoon," but somewhere in their honeycombed brains, their music lies intact and impermeable. Wow!

APRIL
MAY
JUNE

June 13, 2003

My niece, Jackie lives near Seattle. She, too, pictures Grandma much differ-ently from this old woman I visit here in Florence. Busy as she is with one-year-old twins, Jackie takes time to write. She, too, emails me for reports and to express love and concern.

Hi Sweet Niece,

Your Grandma is doing very well. She doesn't really know who I am. It's like her mind has lost depth. She knows that I am James, smiles and wants to hold hands, yet doesn't remember much else. She has reached a blessed place, where living isn't painful because the memories are gone. She is quick to smile and looks like an old bone of a woman. She still picks on the staff, which makes them smile, and eats so slowly that lunch is being served when she is finishing the last of her breakfast. Her body doesn't seem to cause her pain. She has suffered rashes from her diapers. It's funny how we start off our lives with disposables and end it the same way. I love having her close. When I look in her eyes, I still see the love she has always had for her children and grandchildren. I need to get back to work, Sweet One. Write and tell me about the wonders of your life.

Uncle James

JULY
AUGUST"
SEPTEMBER

September 3, 2003

There is a keypad on the fence next to the gate that has a magnetic lock. The gate is part of a security system of metal fencing that encloses the small yard behind Mom's building. The clients wandering off and getting lost or hurt is a concern for the management and this is how they make a little of the outdoors available, yet keep everyone safe.

Mom is always easy to spot. She kept sticking her hands through the spokes of her wheel chair and the staff taped cardboard over the wheels to protect her hands and arms. Seeing their temporary repair I purchased a couple of purple snow dishes and cut them down to the size of her chair's wheels. I attached them with those zip plastic ties, and "zap" safe hands. The large purple discs keep her different than the rest of the patients.

Today she is sitting in the dining area and is slumped forward. At first glance you would think she was reaching for something on the floor, but she isn't. I sit in the chair in front of her and she, without changing her expression, looks up at me. I let a minute or two pass before I greet her with a "Hi, Mom!" I think she would have continued her bland stare endlessly without my greeting. "Oh! How did you find me?" was her question. She knows I am someone, but isn't sure who. I tell her who I am, and she gives me her but-of-course smile and squeezes my hand. A sparkle drifts across her eyes and we visit. Visiting is hard lately. Mom starts to talk and then her voice slips into a soft, low sound that is beyond my ability to hear. I pat her hand and smile. "Yes, Mom. How was that for you? Did you have fun? Who did you meet?" I ask these questions when her slow muttering stops, and she smiles and goes on. Her legs have sat too long. They don't straighten out. I put her feet on the seat of my chair and rub the back of her bent legs. They are tight, and I don't think she will stand again. After a while I stand, promising to be back in a few minutes. She pats my hand and says "OK!" When I tell her I love her she always looks me in the eye, and with her tears a breath away says, "I love you, Honey."

September 24, 2003

Dear Judy,

The days are shorter and the leaves are starting to change. A few have dropped with a promise of more in the weeks to come. I have had more time to visit with Mom. I am unimpressed with her willingness or ability to release the bend in her legs. She, according to Suzanne, gives me the evil grimace when I pick up her feet and place them on the seat of my chair. I rub her knees and the backs of her legs and she doesn't relax. I keep it a part of our visits and she seems OK with it but I, until Suzanne visited with me, didn't know about the face making. She is also taking to holding my thumb and squeezing as hard and as long as she can. She loves the power of it all. I love it that she is still full of fight.

We start our visit with my popping a Tootsie Roll Pop into her mouth. She loves it and won't remove it until it is gone. I have pulled and pulled on the stick without success. We got down to only brown ones before I refilled her supply and started giving her the orange and red ones she loves. Talking has been poor for some time, and the sucker doesn't improve that end of the visit. I like the gentle place Mom is in. She raises her voice and talks to some of the nosier clients from time to time, then spends the balance of her visit looking at me with her Mother Teresa eyes and squeezing my thumb. Suzanne and I are looking forward to your visit. I love you sweet sister,

James

September 26, 2003

As we walked Mom would raise her hands over her shoulder to hold my hand. I would stop pushing, hold her, give her a little kiss and stand as she pulled my hand against her cheek and kissed it. "You are a good guy," she would whisper. During all the blocks I pushed her chair, those were the only words I heard. She would raise her hand and point at a home, or a fence, or some one's pile of firewood as we walked through the neighborhood around Elderberry Square.

I had been sitting in my office and could see that it was an exceptional morning. I had been reading a note I had written about Mom and decided that I wanted to be with her. It's only a few minutes drive to Elderberry Square, and I was caught up on my work. It's hard to escape during the busy months of summer, but as autumn sets in and business slows, I am finding pleasure in leisure visiting, rather than the pressed feelings of grabbing short moments during my busy weeks.

I grabbed the foot brackets for Mom's chair, her coat, and was by her side making the changes before she had a chance to recognize me. Getting out the door was the most difficult part of our mid-morning escape. Elderberry Square has a built in security system. Each of the patients wears a bracelet that emits a signal to the door. The doors lock when patients are close by, so I have to park Mom fifteen feet from the door, shoo the other patients into the TV room, and open the door, leaving a wedge in it to keep it from closing. I then grab Mom, roll her through the door, kicking out the wedge on my way by. When the door closes and latches, I know that all the other mothers are safe from wandering away.

We spent our lovely hour walking and stopping. I know, even though there weren't words, that Mom was enjoying herself. She has always been attracted to creativity and beauty. When we returned, I sat on the sofa and gave Mom her Tootsie Roll Pop. We held hands and I watched the room filled with Mom's fellow patients. It was very, very quiet. At the round table beside the big window four women sat an equal distance from each other. They all moved slowly like a German clock with a spring close to unwound. There were no words, smiles or rapid movements. These women were all walkers and in better shape than Mom. A long time passed, and all I heard was the distant sound of the TV and the occasional squeak of an unoiled wheelchair moving an inch forward or backwards.

From the hall, I heard the voice of one lady who walks and walks and walks. She was saying, "Hay dee dee dee dee hay." She repeated her chant over and over as she walked beside another lady in a wheelchair. Taking a minute or two to cover four floor tiles the lady in the chair rolled up to the big round table and stopped beside one of the women. They looked at each other for several minutes without moving their heads and turning only their eyes in each other's direction. I then heard a deep woman's voice, deeper than many men's, say so softly that I was barely able to hear, "Get the hell away from me." No one moved. I stayed for another five or ten minutes, while the women, with their heads still unturned, stared at each other without blinking.

OCTOBER

October 18, 2003

My relationship with Mom has changed from living beside the ocean with all the weather coastal living can bring, to a small calm lake sheltered by tall pines. It is most always the same. I have taken to entering Elderberry Square through the back courtyard, due to the ease in its simple security system. It also gives me a chance to pop into her room and assure myself that every thing is clean and in order.

The Elderberry Square staff does a wonderful job of keeping their facility and the patient rooms clean and fresh. With all of Mom's pictures on the walls and her personal room furniture, it has a home feeling. Further down the long hall is the dining area where I usually find Mom. She is easy to spot with the large purple discs on her wheelchair wheels. The discs do a good job of protecting her fingers when she dangles her hands beside the wheels and another patient rolls her. Before the discs she would hurt her hands when they were in the spokes and she got a surprise roll. Mom is very slow in recognizing me. I can sit down in a chair, roll her between my legs and hold her hands and place our faces a foot apart without her knowing who I am. If I add my voice with a, "Good morning, Mom. How are you?" We will probably connect. Not always. When the connection is made, she is very sweet and puckers up for a kiss. She then starts talking slow and very softly. I can understand very little, and content myself with rubbing the back of her hands and laughing when she looks up at me and smiles. This is what we do until it is time to leave. I always promise to return in a little bit and ask, "Will you be here when I come back, Mom?" She says, "Yes," and I kiss her goodbye.

October 20, 2003

In this odyssey of Alzheimer's, help comes from unexpected sources. As difficult as this is for our family, Mom's illness has afforded us opportunities to express appreciation to many who don't even know they are helping us through hard times. Here is an example:

Dear Tootsie Roll Pops Manufacturers,

The purpose of this letter is to share my appreciation for your product and its healing powers. I was raised in a home where Tootsie Roll Pops were a special treat for good behavior. My favorite flavor was the chocolate, closely followed by orange. My mother was known to share in our appreciation of your good lollipops.

Many years have passed and my mother is now eighty-four years old and suffers from Alzheimer's. She lives in a Care Center and is not very connected to the real world. She does however, remember Tootsie Roll Pops. I ensure a pleasurable visit with her by arriving with one in my hand. With her lollipop in her mouth, she and I sit while she smiles and pats the back of my hands and sucks away.

On an all too regular a basis, Mom slides into high anxiety. Her doctor has prescribed drugs that calm her down and leave her very disconnected from the world for days. I stocked her bedroom with your product, and asked the staff to give her one when she was anxious to see if she would calm and not have to take the disabling drugs. They have been popping Pops instead of drugs with great success.

Thanks for making my Mom's life better,

James Heintz

October 31, 2003

Judy and Mag were down for a few days. On Halloween, we were visiting with Mom when it became apparent we had a little problem. Mom was coming on to Mag, her son-in-law of 40 years, and although he was a good sport, it was apparent some discomfort was in place. "No, no you are not going to move," she said as she held his arm and growled. I don't think I have ever heard Mom growl before. Mag made several attempts to escape and Mom would say, "Not without me."

Judy had purchased a couple of black and orange cakes with a tub of ice cream to treat all the staff and patients. She was informed by the kitchen staff that everyone had already eaten lots of sugar. They didn't want us to add more to their already overloaded systems. We dished it up for us and, from time to time, we would be visited by a bright-eyed patient wanting a little bite. We would quickly glance around the room, then we would sneak them a little bit, and then shoo them off.

We had an interesting side adventure as Patricia and Maggie, two fellow patients of Mom, fought over the only love seat in the dining area. Both women are nonverbal and are creative in getting their way. Today Patricia was sitting on the small sofa and Maggie was unwilling to share it with her. Maggie slowly, because she can't move quickly, sat on Patricia's lap. She sat there for the longest time wiggling from side to side as they both pretended that nothing was happening. After more than a handful of minutes, Maggie gave up and shared the love seat with Patricia. Patricia had acted poised and content throughout Maggie's harassment.

NOVEMBER

November 13, 2003

It was a couple of hours after Mom's lunch when I walked down the hall towards the dining room. Mom was in the little hall that ties the front and dining rooms to the long sleeping corridor. The building's U shape gives the patients, who like walking, lots of carpet miles to cover. I enjoy visiting with Mom later in the day when she is all cleaned up from her lunch, which has become a bit of a mess. As hard as I try, I don't like watching Mom eat with her hands. She raised me differently than that, and I don't seem to think it's OK for her to break her own rules. I appreciate that there isn't a lot of logic in my position, but I guess that is how it is.

Mom was an exceptional sight today. The staff had dug out a box of old silk flowers so the ladies could make some flower arrangements. Mom had found a string of yellow spring flowers separated by bright blue beads that she had wrapped around her head. She kind of looked like a spring bride. When she spotted me and completed her prolonged, "Who is that guy process," she smiled and clapped her hands. I pulled up a chair and pulled her wheelchair between my legs so I could hold her hands.

We talked about the funny stuff that grows on her skin and she pulled my goatee and laughed at my gray hair. There were several times I caught her looking at me with a questioning look and knew she was wondering if I was my father or not. The staff gave me an update on her behavior. They told me that yesterday she was filled with tears and had escalated in her sadness until they gave her meds. "We just can't let her cry for hours and hours," was the aide's statement. I wondered later if the Tootsie Roll Pop treatment would have worked, or if they even tried it.

November 19, 2003

We have had a big change in our weather and are now in the middle of a three-day winter storm. Judy and I are in the process of making holiday plans for Thanksgiving. Suzanne and I will leave Florence early Saturday and arrive in Sacramento in time for dinner. Mom will be on her own this time. It probably won't matter. Judy and I have both noticed that another change is slinking up on Mom. Her continued bliss has been interrupted with tearful days. I have enjoyed her for months and have found many moments of quality time between us.

Yesterday, a little before lunch, I found Mom in the front room where she and eight or nine other women were sitting and participating in exercise. The instructor had them stretching with scarves in their hands. Mom, when she spotted my watching, put on a show. She did her hoochie coochie routine and made her *"aren't I beautiful"* facial expressions. She tickled me.

She wasn't sure who I was, but was happy to hold my hand until they made the call for lunch. I rolled her to the dining room and turned her over to one of the aides for a visit to the potty before her lunch.

DECEMBER
JANUARY

January 2, 2004

The ground around Elderberry Square is covered with snow. Snow is very rare in Florence. I am anxious to visit with Mom to see if she has noticed. So many of her winter days in Yakima had snow covered yards.

Judy and I are both pleased with Mom's condition. She most always is pleasant and likes to hold hands while she shares in her half sentence disconnected thoughts, which she caps off with smiles. We start with, "Hi, Mom. How are you?" After a long pause and her eyes full search of my face, she responds with, "Oh, it is you, Honey. How did you find me?"

We hold hands and sit. From time to time she will drop my hand and roll off to check the halls. I have become part of the room and her attention is drawn in other directions. I end our visit with, "I have a meeting, Mom, and will be back in a little bit. Is that OK? She responds with her, "Just for a little bit?" I say, "Ya, Mom, I will be back in a few minutes." She says, "OK, Honey. I will wait here for you."

FEBRUARY

February 18, 2004

It's all the same anymore. I park in the lot and punch the code into the back gate. The cyclone fence swings open and I walk along behind the buildings, up the ramp and into the door on the back of Mom's wing. She is never in her room. I usually find her in the dining room or in the hall. She never goes to the TV room. I remember her disliking the television when Dad was alive. "Not much worth watching anymore," were her words back then. She probably feels the same today.

I found her in the hall today, and I stood beside her for a minute. She glanced up at me without changing her bland expression and then, without a note of recognition, looked back down the hall she was rolling. I stepped in front of her chair and squatted down. "Hi, Mom! How are you?" She elevated her head forward and looked closer as she greeted me. "Hi, Honey." "Do you have time for a little visit?" I asked as I spun her around and moved towards the dining room. We talked for a little bit. She didn't finish any of her thoughts and smiled a lot as she reached out and touched my face. I told her I loved her. That is always a mistake. She cries and talks of it not being right, her not having her family. I felt very tender towards her today. She wants a young husband and her three children in her little home on Fourteenth Street. She doesn't remember Dad's name or the home she lived in, but does remember the important feelings she had as a Mom with kids to raise and a husband to love.

MARCH
APRIL

April 09, 2004

Dear James,

Easter wishes to you and all the family. How is your mother doing? I get lazy in writing. Patrick writes email for me. I am just fine and able to do all that needs to be done in my yard and house. Patrick helps on weekends. Love to all,

Aunt Teresa

April 10, 2004

My Dear Aunt Teresa (my Dad's ninety two year old sister),

I wish a very happy Easter to you and Patrick. Mom is thin like a rail and her skin is transparent. Her spirits are high and a smile is often on her face. I have two dear lady friends that are members of the Baha'i Faith and have taken Mom under their wings and visit with her daily. They take her on walks, clip her nails, comb and cut her hair, help her with make-up and hold her hands. They both wanted to give this attention to their moms when they were old and couldn't. They find Mom delightful and it makes them both feel good. Love to you,

James Heintz.

MAY 2004
JUNE 2004
JULY 2004

July 31, 2004

Sweet Jackie,

She looks very old now. She spends her days in a wheel chair and weighs little. She is a bone of a woman who has maintained the ability to smile and laugh. Her legs are frozen at 90 degrees and will not straighten out at her will or the will of her physical therapist. She moves herself about with a custom foot movement you see often where old folks live. She is very slow to remember my name, and holds my hand tightly, unsure if she knows me or not. Pain is not a part of her life although sadness captures her heart in the late afternoon and tears flow. She told Judy that she knows about her tears and times of sadness, but it's OK, and Judy shouldn't be concerned. It would be a true kindness if God chose to claim her. There is so little left of your grandmother and my mother except her smile and her powerful will.

Uncle James

AUGUST
SEPTEMBER
OCTOBER
NOVEMBER
DECEMBER

December 8, 2004

Sometimes she knows me and sometimes she doesn't. She is always pleased to hold my hand and park her wheelchair close to me. Our friend Marcia spends lots of time with Mom and keeps her pretty. Yesterday when I popped in for a visit I found her at Mom's feet trimming her toenails.

Judy and I are very pleased to have Marcia in Mom's life. She spends an hour with her most every morning and watches over her. If a bump or cut appears, she is talking with the staff to find out what happened and what care she is receiving. Mom can never remember Marcia's name.

Lots of folks have come and gone at Elderberry Square, and Mom keeps going. I don't find myself spending much time with her, maybe a short visit a couple of times a week. Although she is content while we visit, my comings and goings don't seem to matter.

JANUARY 2005
FEBRUARY 2005
MARCH 2005

March 17, 2005

"OK Marcia, thanks for the call." Marcia, who visits Mom most every day, had reported that she wasn't able to see Mom today. When she went by Mom was asleep in her bed and had a slight fever. I promised Marcia that I would check her out later tonight. Even though Judy and I have hired Marcia, who is a retired RN, to keep a professional eye on Mom, I some how feel accountable to her. It's funny how that has worked out.

It was close to 7:00 p.m. when I pulled into the Elderberry Square parking lot and decided that I would have to enter the front door rather than the rear entrance, which has the chain link fence with the electronic lock assembly. After several years of the same code they made a change and I didn't remember it. None of the clients were around the electronically secured front door, so I walked in.

My visits are most often during the day. The energy at night is very different. There were a few of the old gals sitting here or there, waiting their turn to be wrapped up in their beds and tucked away. One of the new staff members started to question before she recognized me and said, "Oh, Virginia's son." I was glad for the vigilance.

Mom's door was open and the lights were low. The rails were up on the sides of her bed and they had tucked white pillows up and down the sides of the bed with a large laced one above her head. "Shit!" I thought as I stopped mid-stride and recomposed myself. With her glasses off, hair pulled back away from her forehead, teeth removed and her eyes closed she looked to be in her coffin in some poorly furnished viewing room.

She groaned a little and I exhaled as I drew closer. "Hi, Mom! It's James." She slowly turned her head in my direction and muttered something I didn't understand. I took up her skin and bone hand and kissed her warm skin. She smiled a little and looked at me. Sometimes, I don't know why, her eyes look dark and matted. Their lightness is gone and what is there I don't know and feel uncomfortable in her stare.

I knelt beside her bed and hummed "Home on the Range" as we didn't talk and shared time together. A new aide popped into Mom's room and began displaying how loved Mom is by her and what a special relationship they have. I have found that often new staff members feel this is a part of their jobs when family is around. "Virginia just loves it when I pinch her cheeks," she said. I thought as I stepped back and allowed her to love on Mom that if my mother had more control over her circumstances she would bite her, or possibly punch her in her nose.

I was comfortable that she was OK, took my leave and gave Judy a call on the phone to share my visit.

APRIL

April 5, 2005

Under the broad brimmed straw hat where the face of a farm girl, her arms filled with fresh flowers should have been, I found my mother and the remains of her mind. The appearance of the hat and its placement on her head is a mystery, while the class to wear it and tilt it just so was not.

A fresh spring smile on any face would flatter the floppy edges of the hat's straw brim, while the face I saw, with its withered and twisted lips, rejected the season and captured the loss and discomfort of winter's gloom.

With cheer and high spirits I seized her hands while she growled, protested and pushed me away. With her cheeks in my grasp and a kiss on her lips she paused her assault and withdrew her kick. "Hello, Sweet Mother! Do you know who I am? I'm your son, and I love you as much as I can."

With her eyes more angry than filled with fear, she tilted back her head and squinted her eyes, as she examined me and searched her mind. She paused with a smile and grabbed both my hands. Her head she tilted and her brow she drew down as she said in a whisper, "Who are you, Old Man?"

MAY

May 4, 2005

The e-mail message from my brother's daughter, Jackie, was great news. Her sister, Erica, has given birth to her first child. His name is Aidan and he is very welcome. There was no news about Aidan's mama, which means all is well. One of the strengths the women in this family share is good mothering. Aidan is a lucky boy.

With thoughts of this new life in our family I went to visit my Mama. It is rare that I visit early in the morning and I found her, with all the other women, in the dinning room. She had sweetbread crumbs on her lips and lap mixed with warm mush. The mixture had the initial appearance of some kind of delightful cookie until gravity thinned it out and it slid down the side of her leg to puddle on the seat of her wheelchair.

My priorities have been poor lately and my visits with Mom too rare. When I sat beside her she locked her eyes with mine and without words admonished me. I began our visit with an apology, and with a nod of her head and a pat on the back of my hand, I was, as I have been my entire life, forgiven.

Two weeks ago the doctor ordered a med adjustment for Mom in hopes of happier days for her and the staff that cares for her. This morning the change was obvious. Although she had difficulty completing her long sentences, she had clarity of thoughts, and enjoyably reminisced about her days as a young mother and her joy in being a mom.

I sat on an end table behind Mom's chair and put my chin on her shoulder. She likes the closeness and it is easy to talk when our heads are perched together like two pumpkins sitting on a wall. I enjoyed the intimacy while she finished her breakfast and when I bit her on her shoulder following her teasing me she responded with "That's kind of sexy." Oops. I moved to the chair beside her and shortly kissed her goodbye and promised to return tomorrow.

May 10, 2005

A knot, the size of a bowling ball, is wedged in my gut. My lungs can't fill and the muscles across my shoulders are drawn and twisted. I thought I was angry, but I am anguishing.

While transporting a friend to a dinner, my cell phone rang and Elderberry Square was on the line about my mother. It seems she is not well. She is slumped in her chair with a high temperature and her blood pressure is high. They have called an ambulance and will have her transported to the hospital.

I delivered my friend home from the dinner and drove to the care facility to discover the ambulance lights and the ramp down to transport. "Why is this happening without my OK? Who made the decision?" were the questions that were roaring through my chest and head as I entered the building. Mom was screaming as they lifted her out of her chair and placed her on the gurney.

May 11, 2005

Mom's trip to the hospital was very unnecessary. She had another bladder infection and ended up being prescribed another heavy dose of antibiotics. The staff on duty didn't know Mom's history and were fearful that she was in big trouble, so they played it safe and transported her to the hospital. It takes a lot out of Mom and me when we make these hospital trips. Judy and I have completed all the paperwork for medical directives to keep Mom from being inadvertently in the hospital and hooked up to life support systems that might prolong her life and put us in the uncomfortable position to make life or death decisions that we don't want to be forced into making. We agree that Mom's quality of life isn't much and her pains are many. We are ready to let her go. Getting to this point has been excruciating, so I am angry that our wishes have been disregarded.

JUNE

July 2, 2005

Time continues to pass and my presence beside my Mother must matter on some level. My visits are quiet times of hand holding and little questions. "How is your family? How did you find me? Where do you live now?"

She looks at me through glazed eyes and yet I know she sees. A transparent drape keeps me away and apart from her. My visits are less and my connections with her are thin and ending. Somewhere beyond her body she must be holding up, whole and awaiting her escape. So as she waits I hold her hands and answer her questions.

JULY
AUGUST
SEPTEMBER

September 16, 2005

"She has a cold and is in bed James," were the aide's words as I walked through the dining room and down the hall to Mom's room. "She just doesn't have any energy." I opened the door and saw her on her side with the rails up. Her face was towards the window and she wasn't moving. I walked to the other side of her bed and knelt down to see her face. Her eyes were half open with red half laced lids and her pillowcase was soaked with tears. "How are ya, Mama?" I asked in a soft voice. Her open eyes slowly rolled to me and her wispy voice answered. "It's too hard … It's too hard."

September 22, 2005

My sister and I have talked a lot lately about Mom. The last few visits have ended with "please take me home." She doesn't say it with much hope and quickly wilts back into her wheelchair when I kiss her and say goodbye. I find myself wondering if I could take her home. I want to believe that she would be happy and would sit on our deck and watch the wind and birds whip through the trees. I dream many delightful circumstances where she is with me and happy…. happy in her being with me and happy in my home.

These thoughts of mine are much like thinking about past marriages and how they could have been great if only. The "if only" seems to be the problem. What Mom wants isn't. She can't walk, she can't remember or speak a full sentence. She can't cook let alone feed herself. Her husband and son are dead like most of her friends and family. Judy and I don't have the strength, time or energy to care for her aged body, and I can't endure the heartache of her tears.

Judy and Suzanne both shake their heads when I have these thoughts and remind me of the immense emotional and physical demands involved in caring for Mom. I just wish her days could be filled with more than tears and boredom. She deserves better.

OCTOBER
NOVEMBER

November 30, 2005

It's my sixty-first birthday today. Mom doesn't remember. Something is wrong. They have her propped in her chair. She probably has a bladder infection. They told me that they have had her on antibiotics for a couple of days. I miss Mom.

11

MOM'S LAST DAYS

The 7th stage of the seven stages of Alzheimer's disease identified by the Alzheimer's Association was reached by our Mother during these last days.

Stage 7 Very severe cognitive decline (Severe or late-stage Alzheimer's disease)

This is the final stage of the disease when individuals lose the ability to respond to their environment, the ability to speak and, ultimately, the ability to control movement.

- Frequently individuals lose their capacity for recognizable speech, although words or phrases may occasionally be uttered.
- Individuals need help with eating and toileting and there is general incontinence of urine.
- Individuals lose the ability to walk without assistance, then the ability to sit without support, the ability to smile, and the ability to hold their head up. Reflexes become abnormal and muscles grow rigid. Swallowing is impaired.

DECEMBER

December 3, 2005

Mom had a stroke, or something, five days ago. It changed things a lot. She doesn't talk, eat or have much response to her environment. Judy and I agreed to let her go and contacted the hospice folks. We were lucky and with the help of her doctor, who made a home visit to Elderberry, we are now in a comfort only program.

She seems to be in pain. The hospice folks are giving her morphine every two hours. Sometimes they give her more. It appears that she is in bed now until she dies. There have been many times I thought she was on her deathbed over these past five years.

The first couple of days after her stroke the staff got her up and placed her in her wheel chair. It was sad to see her all slumped over against the pillows they wedged into her chair. Judy and I decided that that wasn't OK and I wrote a note on her chair and room door telling the staff to leave her in bed. She has been a good woman and deserves death in a clean and comfortable bed. It's time to stop saving her life.

I have spent a lot of time with Mom these past days. I talk to her and pray for her. I tell her that its time for her to let go and join Dad, her brother, Steve and her Mama and Dad. I don't think she's going to do it my way. What a surprise. I have always felt that Mom fears her death and she may hang on longer than she should.

I went by the funeral home yesterday to refresh our requests and did some other business around Mom's dying. I was solid in my feelings and without tears. When the hospice nurse said that she thought Mom's death was very close, I found myself alone in the bathroom crying. I feel sorry for myself. I'm going to be an orphan.

December 3, 2005

So here we are at the end of it all. I am glad that Mom is close to her escape from her body which has lost its ability to walk, control its bladder and bowels, remember, understand, eat and swallow. All it can do at its end is breathe and keep its heart beating.

It's hard to look at her all used up. I remember so much and am thankful for everything Mom gave me through her body. She made, nurtured, loved, educated, trained and devoted her life to me and now she is almost done.

December 5, 2005

I've been told that it is important to be with those you love when they die, important for them and for the family. I decided that I wanted to sit with Mom and have been beside her bed for thirty-two hours now. I remain committed to my goal.

I've talked a lot with Judy and my wife, Suzanne, about issues surrounding death. It's been a long time since I have slowed myself down enough to think in depth about it and to wonder about the process.

Mom's stroke, six or seven days ago, ended language for her. What else has ended I don't know. That is what I have been wondering about. She is receiving a little morphine every couple of hours. Before the morphine she seemed confused and would protest if her body was touched; now she seems relaxed and calm. Her breathing is slow and she seems to see without seeing. It's easy to attach a spiritual component to this, but maybe it's all her body being in a shorted-out state and the spiritual stuff will come at her passing. Maybe not!

Judy and I have worked out most of the funeral plans. We don't know when we will put it all in process because it seems Mom will be the one who decide when she's willing to give up living. It does amaze me that after living her past five years, she still wants to hang on to life.

Hospice has been exceptional. The last couple of time we transported her in the handicap taxi for doctor appointments, she got sick. It would take her days to recuperate with lots of vomiting and dry heaves. When we were informed by staff that we would have to transport Mom to the doctor before she could be admitted to hospice, Judy and I were upset and began working the system to avoid moving her. The folks at Elderberry Square were not able to help us out, but the hospice team rallied around us and convinced Mom's physician to do a house visit. Very rare! When Mom's doctor came to her bedside, I deeply thanked him for his willingness to make Mom an exception of his normal practice.

Both of the hospice RN's have spent so much time with us talking about every aspect of the process Mom was moving through. Both of them have been doing hospice work for years and they are like glowing angels. They open the door for everything, including all the feelings that were flowing through me as I moved with Mom towards her death. We talked about Mom's body being unwilling to drink or eat, the protection her body gives as it shuts down, and how she would lose her pangs of hunger. The morphine would drape her with feelings of peacefulness.

I am about to bed down for my second night beside my Mother. Judy and I bought her a recliner several years ago. It probably hasn't be sat in more than ten times and now it is my cot. I wake often and reach out and place my hand on her face and then her neck to see if she is still warm and her heart is beating. Every time I am glad she is still here, and yet very anxious for her to pass.

December 6, 2005

Mom's room has become my space. I spent another night in the recliner and slept through all the visits the staff made. I must have been tired. Jordan called a little after seven for our morning chat while he drove to work. He had to endure all the cold and old man sounds I made as I cleared my head and throat. I've been doing a cold since our trip to Disneyland just before Thanksgiving. I think I caught something on the plane.

Mom and I sound a lot alike first thing in the morning. After a few coughs and a cup of coffee, I return to normal and she doesn't. Last night she was taking about six breaths a minute. This morning is faster at about nine. The staff nurse put her head on Mom's chest and said that her lungs are filling up.

They feed me here. As a matter of fact, they do room delivery. I just finished a plate of bacon and French toast. With my breakfast and a cup of coffee in my system, I am ready for my morning. I called my office and let them know that I wouldn't be in today. I don't want Mom to die alone.

Mom's hands have lost their color and her breath is slight and irregular. Marcia came by late this afternoon and we rolled Mom towards my recliner so I can watch her face. I have turned my head in her direction many times when she missed a breath. The lights are off in the room and it is aglow with the light from the window.

Both the hospice RN and bath woman were in today. The RN said that she couldn't find Mom's heart beat. She said that it was normal at the end.

A couple of old guys, one with a fiddle and the other a guitar are playing music in the dining room. Suzanne brought them down the hall and asked them to play "*Home Home On The Range*." They did and Mom missed a couple of breaths to listen. I like it that in her final hours Mom has her ears filled with live music.

Jamie and Gregg came by this evening to say goodbye. Jamie brought her creams and perfumes which she rubbed on Mom's body. She held Mom's face and told her how much she loved and admired her and that a classy woman like her needed to smell great when she passed.

I told Jamie that I had asked Mom if she would become Jamie's Guardian Angel after she passed. Jamie loved the idea and admitted she could use all the help she could get.

A round and delightful chaplain from the Catholic Church came by and blessed Mom. He read prayers and we talked about her and her life.

Mom is going through all these stages of death. For a while she had a gurgle with mild to rapid breathing. Now she is without noise, very calm and rarely taking a small breath. These past days have been difficult and good for me. Death is such a mystery.

December 7, 2005

It's 2:00 a.m. and she is holding on by a string and won't let go.

It's four in the morning and cold has claimed much of her body. She has a slow breath that is patterned and won't stop. I have held her face and begged her to let go, to join my father and brother, her brother Don. "Don't be afraid, Mama! It will be beautiful and escaping your body will be delightful. Just stop breathing, Mama. Let it go."

The day has moved on and Mom has taken a new turn. Her limbs were cold and now they are warm. Her face and chest are red and flushed. I have a damp cloth on her forehead.

These days beside Mom have been filled with many interesting gifts. I find myself thinking about my father and realizing that I have considered Mom a trust from him. When I think of him standing at the foot of Mom's bed and waiting for her to join him, I find myself asking him, "Did I do OK, Dad?" I want him to turn to me and say, "You bet, Son. You did a good job."

I wanted to take good care of Mom and the struggle of it all has left me wondering. Did I take too good of care of myself at Mom's expense? Could I have endured more of her illness and spent more time with her? Would it have been better for her … for me?

Now with the sunlight in Mom's window, I don't see the figure of my father and I don't have to hear his appraisal of my performance. I know I could have done better.

I painted Mom's nails a few weeks ago a light purple. They match her hands. Who would have guessed?

I am spending hour after hour sitting here watching her breathe. I'm mesmerized. I have noticed that when people come to visit, they do the same thing. You don't need to talk, just sit and watch her. I listen to the changes in her breathing and when she gasps or groans, I freeze. Is this it? Is this the moment? She then takes another breath, and we move on. My cats do the same thing with our DVD player. They will sit for hours waiting for the drawer to open and just about the time they have lost interest the machine makes a click and they are back at attention.

Mom is having a private party inside herself, and we, on the outside, can only guess what she is up to. Did her stroke cleanse her brain and she is without thought? Is she totally aboard and leaning against some part of her interior waiting to float away? Has she stepped aside and is visiting with all her loved ones that have already passed? Does my being here matter? Would she rather be doing this alone? I, along with everyone who visits, can only guess.

An aide that has been gone for the past week came by in the early afternoon to kiss and say, "goodbye" to Mom. She said that Mom would never go to sleep with out her teddy bear in her arms. She walked across the room, picked up a soft foot-tall teddy bear, brought it back and tucked it in close to Mom and wrapped her tired old arms around it. Mom never liked doing anything alone. She seemed to pull the bear in close. We'll never know if that bear became one of her precious children or her husband, but it eased the loneliness and bridged this world with the next. Ten minutes later she passed.

We just sat there for a while. My first breath, which followed her last, was heavy. My lungs felt like old leather bags and I drooped in my chair as I examined her motionless body.

Why we couldn't sit there longer I don't know but the staff started buzzing about and asking questions. Before I had lifted myself from my chair my new friend Allan, from the funeral home, was at my Mother's door with his chrome and red leather gurney. They scooted me out of the room and down the hall as they transferred Mom from her deathbed.

I had talked with the funeral home staff and made them aware of my wishes for Mom's care. Allan told me that I could meet him at the funeral home in an hour and attend to Mom's body.

As I had with my father, I, with my wife Suzanne, bathed Mom and said prayers. I placed rose blossoms on her eyes and left her teddy bear in her arms as we wrapped her in cotton. Later Allan would place her body in a coffin and transport her to Yakima.

December 12, 2005

We all gathered in Yakima, Washington in a little Presbyterian church that my Mom's sister belongs to. The service was small, mostly family and a few friends. We sang the songs, read the prayers, stood and talked about her and then the grandchildren lifted her birch wood coffin and carried her body out of the church.

At the cemetery we all stood in the twenty degree sun filled day and watched the grounds keeper lower the coffin into the freshly dug grave that was next to my father's. We tossed white long stem roses into her burial place, and all took our turns shoveling dirt.

The cemetery has beautiful grass covered hills with ponds, swans and lots of trees. When the frozen sod was packed into place we left and began our drive home to Florence.

Several hours on the road Jamie called. She was sad that she hadn't been able to attend the funeral of her grandmother and wanted to hear every detail. After I shared with her all I could remember, she told me about her dream. She had liked it when I had asked my Mother to watch out for her, to be her Guardian Angel, but didn't give it much more credence than a sweet thought. The night of Mom's death, Jamie found herself dreaming. She was in a new home that had many windows through which the most beautiful golden light flowed, filling the room with bright warmth. She felt peaceful as she walked around the house, and was aware that she needed to move and rearrange things in order to make this house her home. As she began her task the door opened and her Grandmother and Grandfather walked in. She said they were stunning and were so happy and in their love for each other. They looked sixty and were acting forty. The love they shared filled the room and Jamie was delighted to be with them. They were no words only looks of love and acceptance. She said they glided around her and effortlessly moved her things as they, looking back at her, smiled with delight. Without words she knew that they were there to help her change her house into a home. She said that she has never had a dream as real or as beautiful in all her life.

12

PARTING THOUGHTS

Months have passed and I find myself reflecting on the six years I attended to my Mother. Much has changed. My sister and I are orphans. We are also best friends. There were times after Mom's death when I would leave my office and think, as I walked to my car, "Hum, maybe I have time to run by and see Mom." At first I had a hollow feelings, but now it's OK.

I thought that I would want to return to Elderberry Square to check on the staff and the old women Mom had lived with. I haven't and don't think I will. Although they did everything they could to make Mom's life better, my memories of the place are painful. Most of my memories of Mom and the past six years are painful.

Some friends told me the other day that Lolly had died. My last memory of her was she and Mom sitting across from each other in the dinning room calling each other bitches. One would say, "You're a Bitch." The other would respond with, "Am not. You're a Bitch."

I think that memory or the lack of it, pretty well ties up the last six years. I knew Lolly before Alzheimer's and she was an exceptional woman, like my mother. She was high-spirited and artistic. She rode a bicycle around town until she was past 85! Then, she and Mom both were reduced to old and broken women by a disease that showed no mercy.

Now, when I think about Mom, I find that I am starting to bypass the Alzheimer's years and remember better times. Judy says she finds herself doing the same. We have also talked about our fear that some day we may be the patient. What can we tell our children? What words can we say? How can we prepare them?

My hope for all those folks who have Alzheimer's friends and family is that they will be able to protect themselves from this disease. Knowledge and support are of utmost importance.

When I reflect on the question my Mother often asked, "How did you find me?" I think of the thousands of victims of Alzheimer's who become lost in their own brains, and the families that journey with them through that lostness. It is for all of them that I write this book, and, of course, for Mom. Her persistent question has one answer for me. "Mama, I found you wonderful."

EPILOGUE

A couple of weeks ago, while I was shopping in the Safeway store, I bumped into Margaret's daughter, Elizabeth. Margaret had spent the last years of her life with my Mother in the Alzheimer's unit at Elderberry and had died a week or two before Mom. Elizabeth and I were the supportive children who spent a lot of time visiting with and watching over our impaired parents. We had shared conversations in the dinning room when our Moms wandered away from us in their confusion. I asked her if she had ever gone back to visit the staff and patients our parents had left behind. She dropped her head slightly in a shadow of shame and said that she hadn't. She had driven buy many times and couldn't bring herself to turn into the parking lot. I told her that it was the same for me, that I was finding it difficult to even drive by.

We gave each other a hug and separated as we pushed our carts down different aisles.

978-0-595-40461-2
0-595-40461-8